T0210953

The Craft and Science
of Game Design

THE CRAFT AND SCIENCE OF GAME DESIGN

A Video Game Designer's Manual

Phil O'Connor

CRC Press
Taylor & Francis Group
Boca Raton   London   New York

CRC Press is an imprint of the
Taylor & Francis Group, an **informa** business

First edition published 2021
by CRC Press
6000 Broken Sound Parkway NW, Suite 300,
Boca Raton, FL 33487-2742

and by CRC Press
2 Park Square, Milton Park, Abingdon, Oxon, OX14 4RN

© 2021 Taylor & Francis Group, LLC
CRC Press is an imprint of Taylor & Francis Group, LLC

ISBN: 9780367562458 (hbk)
ISBN: 9780367556532 (pbk)
ISBN: 9781003097006 (ebk)

Typeset in Minion Pro
by KnowledgeWorks Global Ltd.

Dedicated to Greg Stafford
(February 9, 1948 – October 10, 2018),
my game design hero, mentor, guide and
shaman for 40 years. Thank you, Greg.

Contents

Acknowledgements

Special thanks go to my wife Kaitlyn for her perspective and sense of humour, her artistic flair and ideas for the illustrations, and to my mother Helene for her early proofreading and editing knowledge that helped form the final manuscript.

CHAPTER 1

An Introduction to Games

INTRODUCTION

While beginning this project, I thought of the title of this book as a way to frame the contents and my subsequent task as a writer. I considered various lofty titles that were quickly discarded, as most first time authors probably do. Going back and forth on a few ideas made me realize what my motivation was for writing on this subject in the first place. Early in my career, I encountered challenges that at first I did not seem to know the solution to. Some of the difficulties of game development seemed incredibly complex and difficult to unravel. I began to reflect about these issues because I loved my work but I did not want to repeat the difficult experiences that seemed to me avoidable if only I understood the cause. After separating process issues from communication and organization, I broke down each set of challenges and collected my own set of lessons-learned into an essay that was later published online. The response to this article was positive at first, but over the ensuing years, it has garnered more attention that I ever expected. Veteran developers have remarked on the accuracy of some of my observations, and people starting out in the field have contacted me about the article and how helpful it was to them.

The sad truth about the game industry is that there seems to be few sources of up-to-date educational material on development, most of us learn on the job and we discover solutions to the same problems that are universal to making video games. As an industry we are in a perpetual adolescence, relearning the same lessons over and over and reinventing the wheel. Though things have improved by a great magnitude since the early days of video games, there still is a general amnesia and much lost knowledge that could spare future developers a lot of difficulty. I hope to reverse this trend to the degree that I can through *The Craft and Science of Game Design*. There is much to gain for the game industry as a whole if we take time to document and share our experiences. If we can make fewer mistakes in the future, development budgets will be easier to control, with fewer failed projects each year and the rate of successful releases might go up. But the main goal is to ease the suffering of my fellow developers and future ones. I love this industry and the process of making video game entertainment for millions of people, but I think as developers we sometimes pay a heavy price in stress, work-life balance and financial stability. I hope this book might, in some small way, reduce the personal cost of game development with a few lessons from my own experiences.

The second reason I wished to write this book is to elevate the reputation of game designers as a discipline. Designers are sometimes considered amateurs, compared to the other disciplines who must train extensively in their field to qualify as artists, programmers, etc. Despite the availability of excellent formal education programs for designers, much of the professional skills required to be an effective designer are learned on the job. Game design is a lot about feelings and emotions, but it is expressed through software which requires scientific methods to translate effectively. The title of this book I believe expresses the essence of video game design work, which requires the artist's craftsmanship and flair, as well as the scientist's methodical approach and empirical objectivity.

This book is not meant to be theoretical or a discussion of game theory or game design techniques, it is more of a set of lessons from personal experience on how to be successful developing games in the role of designer. There are plenty of other books out there that go into abstract design theory and break down most game genres in detail. This is not that kind of book, it is written as a collection of tips, information, background, techniques and hard-earned knowledge from the trenches of game development. It is intended as a practical guide with reference to my first-hand experience on multiple mid to high-end development projects. If you have ever contemplated becoming a video game designer or are studying to become one or have been in the industry for some years, this book will have something for you.

In addition to some background about the craft and science of game design and the role of games in our society, this manual goes into production techniques, documentation, the psychology of development teams, project cycles and the common challenges in game design. It is the kind of manual that I wish was available when I started out, way back in 1990s when I got my first paid job as a professional games maker.

If you aspire to be a designer, or are studying in a program to become one, this book will give you some idea of what to anticipate and hopefully give you a head start on some of the most common challenges and pitfalls of video game development. If you are already a professional designer, it should give you the opportunity to compare your experiences with those described inside, and maybe some pieces will fall into place for your own understanding of this highly complex and challenging field.

The advantage in reading this book is that it contains information on how to be professional within the game development field. In a sense, this information applies to most development- or project-based work, and a lot of it comes from various fields and literature about leadership, psychology and anecdotes from experienced people from all walks of life.

The second source of advice contained herein comes from what they used to call the school of hard knocks. The mistakes I have made have been the most valuable learning experiences; I have learned more from the difficult situations that I have faced rather the easy ones. I believe this is probably most people's experience in life. However, this is not to say that you should seek out bad situations to broaden your experience, on the contrary. But if you are faced with a tough situation, you should look at it from the perspective of learning something from the experience that will make you a better person and game developer in the long run.

DISCLAIMER

This book is written from a personal experience point of view and naturally, it is a biased perspective. All assumptions, generalizations, conclusions and presumptions are mine alone. It is my hope that it can better serve the next generation of game designers as it is written from the point of view of practical examples from my own development experience. As such though, my experience does not cover all types of development projects that are out there today, it mainly focuses on console/PC development. For those looking for wisdom in virtual reality, augmented reality, mobile, social and whatever else will come out in the near future, you might find that most of these tips should still apply but with the caveat that different technologies bring their own unique challenges. Those readers looking to break into those specific sectors may wish to seek additional material on that media; however, the information within these pages should still apply to all designers no matter what platform they are developing for, with a little adaptation and imagination.

BACKGROUND ON THE VIDEO GAME INDUSTRY

The global video game industry is a massively expanding sector of modern entertainment. What began with the development of microchips in the 1970s has expanded into a $150-billion-a-year business according to some global estimates (as of 2020). Some projections for the future predict a growth rate of 5–8% per year. This is definitively a constantly growing entertainment sector, which is increasingly fragmenting across different technologies and financial models.

As a game designer in today's video game industry, the development environment is becoming more complex, especially on the technology side with platforms as varied as social/browser, handhelds, two generations of consoles, tablets, smartphones and finally PC games, to name some of the biggest. In addition, the publishing environment is more complex as well, with self-publishing, crowd funding, free to play and traditional boxed retail all mixed in with a variety of funding models. For today's designers, it is a bit of a jungle out there, learning the ropes of each publishing model and platform is difficult to do in one lifetime. Mastering design within constantly shifting financial and technological conditions will be an ongoing challenge for the professional designer of the future. The good news is that video games have never been in more demand, with approximately 2.7 billion playing games (as of 2020 estimates). That's nearly 33% of all human beings on the planet. Your skill and talents will be in more demand as time goes by, human beings play games by their very nature. They have always done so and always will.

As a student of design and games, it is useful to understand the cultural history of games and the potential biological origins of our relationship with games. This is important to know because the craft and science of game design play out in the mind of your audience, all of your work gears to creating an illusion inside the head of your player; a believable illusion, a very strong and sometimes emotionally powerful illusion. A game designer is not unlike a magician or illusionist if you prefer. You engineer gameplay that takes your player into your game world, you dress it in assets that support your theme and you create incentives for the player to learn about your game. Once you have your audience interested, you entertain them with meaningful choices and rewards for as long as your budget/design allows. If you want to be successful in game design, you must understand your audience above all else. This is where your craft and science lives, in the mind of the player. And the player is both a biological being and a product of their culture. Knowing a bit about both is helpful to being a successful game designer.

Designers already have a clue about what makes a player audience tick. After all, they are human beings themselves, a product of their upbringing, their peer culture and society. Most designers bring this innate understanding of their audience to their work subconsciously, but a more formalized approach is very useful, especially when you are trying to make games that appeal beyond your own personal demographic or cultural region. The best designers are able to break out of their own personal experience (as varied as it may be) to reach into vastly different audiences. In order to be able to do that, it is useful to examine some ideas on human game culture and delve a little into anthropology and psychology.

THE AUDIENCE: THE PLAYER

Designers are entertainers. Game design is not about making a tool or a product that has utility such as buildings, cars or furniture. It is not about making software; it is about making software-based entertainment: video games. This discipline does not require scientific training, unlike an architect whose designs have to meet exact structural, material and functional specifications. Nonetheless, games need to be structurally sound, they must meet the requirements of the technology, the budget and the sales objectives within a production plan (as vague or inconstant as all of those can be at different stages of the project). As a designer, you must manage this vagueness through a

development cycle of variable length with a final entertainment quality objective that can change during the project, and/or be understood differently by different key players in the project. All of this requires a concrete, objective, nearly scientific approach to design to make all of those "squishy parts" of a game project become more solid to the different disciplines that require that concreteness: production, art, programming, level design, marketing, animation, audio, etc.

On the flip side, all the concreteness and rational methodology in the world will not guarantee the success of your game. In the end, the final product is a piece of art, an illusionary experience created by digital technology that allows an audience to play your game as *entertainment in their own mind.* There are few things more subjective than fun, video games are far from being an exception to the rule that beauty (and entertainment) is in the eye of the beholder.

But it's not all illusion. There are standards for visual polish, production values and elegance that all professional designers must understand and apply to any game. There is a minimum quality bar in terms of player feedback, elegance of the interface, smooth gameplay and good visuals. The professional designer knows how much polish they need to bring the entertainment content up to its best quality bar.

Quantifying or taming that subjectivity is possible and indeed essential. The game designers must be able to do this in order to sell their design. The paradox of designing games is that your subject matter is purely notional, subjective and widely interpreted, but game development requires hard facts and concrete pillars on which to build a development project. You can visualize game design as a process of herding ideas towards a final objective, acting as a shepherd for the game. During the process many ideas need to be culled, until only the ones that are relevant and robust are left.

Taming game ideas is easier with a little reflection on the history and social role of gaming in human society. Of all of the human activities, gaming is probably the least studied and understood. There is very little serious academic study of gaming despite its universality in all human cultures, past and present. A student of game design should be curious about the origins of the medium and its possible roots in biology. Much of this section is based on my personal observations, guesswork and a few serious studies on the subject.

THE BIOLOGY OF GAMES

There is very little research on why humans like to play. Psychology and anthropology mostly seems to ignore gaming, perhaps the assumption is that it has little impact on society and is just a leisure pastime.

I would suggest that play is a critically important part of our animal biology and a feature of highly intelligent animals. It is

a central part of our learning mechanism, and is rooted in very ancient instincts that evolved from our earliest mammal ancestors. So let's start from the beginning: animals, do they play? If they do, why?

Everyone who has owned a pet can verify that animals play. Cats play, dogs play and even wild animals play, especially when they are young. An interesting distinction is that play behaviour in animals seems to be mostly exclusive to mammals; the more primitive families of animals do not seem to possess the cognitive ability to play (80% of mammals show play behaviour according to some biology studies). Lizards, being the closest to modern mammals on the evolutionary scale, do not seem to engage in any kind of play behaviour. Why would mammals evolve the ability to engage in play when other animals do not seem to need to? Biologists believe that it is linked to cognitive ability. Mammals are more advanced cognitively on several levels compared to other species; they have social abilities and show bonding behaviour that is more advanced and complex than in other species. They also seem to have more abstract thinking ability than other species. Play behaviour is linked to abstract thought and to social bonding.

You may be asking at this point what animal play behaviour has to with ancient board games and modern video games, and my answer would be: everything. As animals we inherited all our behaviours from a long line of organisms stretching back millions of years in the past. We, as human beings, have been programmed with biological software and hardware that have evolved from a long line of animals that adapted behaviours that would enhance their chances of survival over millions of years. Play behaviour is clearly an adaptation that gave mammals a survival advantage. We have inherited this characteristic from our mammal ancestors, and this is possibly one of the key reasons behind our advanced intelligence.

Play behaviour is a learning and social mechanism. Animals play to learn how to use their bodies, practice their skills and test each other in social games that help them become stronger and smarter, and bond them as a group. This is easily observable especially in young mammals who seem to spend a lot of time playing, just as our children do.

If it isn't already obvious, as mammals we share play behaviour, both as children and well into adulthood. It appears to play a role in our intelligence and our ability to learn, it brings us together socially and it teaches us how to analyse complex situations and devise stratagems. It also allows us to develop high-performance skills, a process that we seem to find satisfying. Each species exhibits a different style of playing, but it is all linked to survival. If you look closely, you will see "biologically" different games for each type of mammal species. Dogs play games of chase, tug of war and fetch, hunting skills. Cats attack anything that seems to move, as if they were perpetually chasing an abstract mouse of their own imagining. These play behaviours are linked to dog survival and cat survival, and our play behaviour also developed from that need to train for survival, which is probably the reason behind the high-stress situations that we enjoy in our video games.

The conclusion I think we can draw from looking into the biology of play is that we as human beings are natural born players; play behaviour in mammals is linked to better being able to cope with survival and this instinct is so strong that animals engage in cross-species play. We play with our pets and even wild animals have been observed to play with each other even in prey-predator situations. A casual search online can yield a bunch of amusing videos showing animals at play, even a polar bear playing with some huskies.

What this means for the game designer is humans are instinctively wired to play, and it is linked to learning and self-improvement. A designer is both an entertainer and a teacher; if you can bring these elements into your game, you can tap into the subconscious desire of all human beings to learn and achieve.

THE CULTURAL ORIGINS OF GAMING

Video games may seem to be a relatively new medium, a product of the digital age, but if you go back into the furthest depths of recorded history, you will find that playing games is one of the oldest human activities since the dawn of civilization, right alongside agriculture, art, music and architecture. Archaeologists

have discovered evidence that board games predate the invention of writing. The oldest known board game is Senet and it was discovered in Egyptian tombs that are over 5000 years old. It seemed to fulfil both a religious and entertainment function. It is believed that Senet was about souls crossing the underworld, and two players took turns throwing dice sticks and moving their pieces through a series of tiles to reach the end. We will come back to the religious aspect later on in this chapter, as it seems twivilizations have engaged in games for spiritual purposes as well as leisure.

The oldest board game for which the original rules are known is considered to be The Royal Game of Ur (Figure 1.1); a game that has survived to this day in its current form as Backgammon. The oldest set of board and pieces was found in tombs excavated in the 1920s, in the city of Ur, by Sir Leonard Woolley, dated to around 2700 BC.

The game was referred to as the "Game of 20 Squares" (Figure 1.2) in the rules, which were discovered in Cuneiform

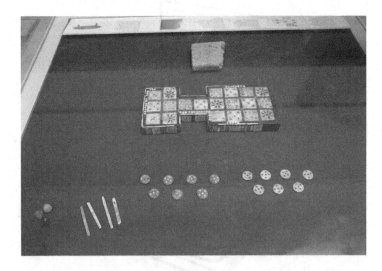

FIGURE 1.1 The oldest board game in the world, the Royal Game of Ur.

FIGURE 1.2   Rules for Game of 20 Squares, dated 177 BC. Game design is an old profession. (Courtesy of the British Museum.)

text tablets excavated in Mesopotamia (see below). These game rules represent the earliest game designs recorded. Though the Egyptian game of Senet is thought to be up to 900 years older, its rules in written form have not survived to this day.

Another contender for the oldest game known is Mancala, which is dated to between 7000 BC and 5000 BC based on recent National Geographic excavations in modern Jordan. Some pictures of Mancala are shown further along in the text (below). Mancala was played with stones and boards made of rows of depressions carved directly on rocks. They can be found all around the ancient city of Petra, and several versions of it seem to have been popular with the Nabataean people.

These discoveries suggest game design is one of the oldest professions, or at least if not yet a profession, had a social function from the dawn of civilization. Right there at the very beginning of civilized society, when writing was developed to organize government, the economy, science and art, it was also being used to design games. It makes you wonder how many game designs will never be known to us.

A casual search through ancient history will reveal nearly all early civilizations had some sort of popular game that reflected the culture of its people. The universality of games in history and their early appearance in the archaeological record suggest that gaming is very important to human society; the concept of leisure games is almost synonymous with civilization. And I mean specifically games that require playing, pieces, a board, strategic thinking and intellectual reasoning. They are distinctly different from the multitude of other games people have always played such as games of chance or gambling, games that involve team sports, games of physical contests such as the Olympic games and games that pit combatants in a test of martial skill, all of which are just other aspects of the human compulsion to play games of every sort.

There are other examples that show gaming has been part of human culture since the dawn of civilization. In ancient Mohenjo-Daro, a city that gives its name to the otherwise unknown ancient civilization of the Indus Valley, archaeologists have excavated playing pieces and dice as well as rooms that were seemingly reserved for playing board games (Figure 1.3). It is believed that the ancient game of Chaturanga, (or "Four Parts", a precursor of modern chess) was played socially by an important part of the population in areas reserved for gaming. That means that the earliest known cities had specifically designated buildings or spaces for people to play games.

FIGURE 1.3   4000 year old playing pieces.

If we look at other ancient cultures, we find the same pattern: Ancient Greeks, Maya, Phoenicia, Africa, China, etc., all had some form of cultural gaming tradition that proved to be very old and long lived.

What does it mean to modern students of game design that the archaeological record shows a near-universal prevalence of people playing games socially from the dawn of civilization? My conclusion is that gaming must be a deep part of the makeup of the human mind, it is in our blood, it is part of our nature to seek out and play games that are abstract models of strategy, skill and chance. I believe this is so because games serve a variety of functions for human beings. We are gaming primates, down to the core.

First, the social function, games bring people together and in playing games, we form language and ideas around them. We bond around games, we spend our leisure time together, we are entertained and we engage in a pastime that in some cases is a strong aspect of the culture that we participate in. As an example, the game of GO in China is near legendary as a deep part of the identity of Chinese culture and a demonstration of some of its philosophical principles.

Second reason why I believe we like to play games is to show our skill and be recognized for it by our peers. As an example of how important games can be to personal prestige, look at the celebrated grand masters of Chess and the endless debates and discussions about their strategies and moves. Many famous figures in history were notoriously good players of their cultural game.

A third reason is some games act as inspiration, they invite the player to meditate on the lessons and strategy of the game which can mirror the struggles of life. Games are often an abstraction of the world around us and invite the player to use the same thought processes that are useful in our day-to-day life. Games that require planning, strategizing and logic to win use the same complex skills we apply to get through life.

Finally, I believe that humans are naturally competitive, and pitting our wits against our friends and peers is inherently pleasurable. Competition connects us to our peer group, gives us a moment of triumph or two so we can show others our special talent, and builds our confidence and abilities. Even losing forces one to evaluate the reasons for the loss and to improve oneself, eventually achieving proficiency. Friendly competition is a social safety valve, a way to ease personal pressures and focus competitive urges positively.

Human beings like playing games; they fulfil an important role in our society, as important as art, dance, literature, music and all the other forms of human expression.

These ancient board games are directly linked to the modern hobby of video games because they are representations of abstract systems designed to put one player in a contest of logic and chance against another player. Our modern technology has allowed us to replace the other player with artificial intelligence (AI) or link one player to a multitude of others, but the essence of the entertainment value remains the same. We like using our decision-making skills, coordination, reasoning and prediction powers in abstract contests under intense pressure, for the pure joy of entertainment. But video games are not just modern board games, they are far from it.

STORYTELLING

Human beings are communication champions; our societies are built on communication and exchange of ideas. One of the means through which we bond as a group and exchange complex cultural ideas is through storytelling. Human beings have been telling each other stories for millennia, before civilization existed or even the invention of farming, we have gathered to tell each other stories. The psychology of storytelling is probably a very

lengthy and fascinating discussion but for the purposes of how it relates to video games, game designers are modern storytellers. This very old human instinct to create and transmit stories lives on in our modern world through video games and people become just as passionate about the stories they tell. Technology is the only difference with how and where we tell these stories, but the stories are the same.

The value of storytelling goes beyond the social bonding and shared sense of culture and community; stories tell us universal truths, give us cautionary tales, allow us to think about complex emotions and possibilities without having to live them out fully. Stories bring us together and bond us to the teller. Each of us has stories to tell, and as a video game designer, you get to tell a few of your own to a huge audience. The player is not only the audience but also a participant in the stories we tell; they get to be the subject of the story, make changes to it and sometimes decide how it ends. It's a very rewarding and fulfilling vocation in the tradition of the ancient poets and bards that used to travel around communities spreading news and entertaining.

In the modern age, we have given that role over to movies, TV, books, theatre, tabletop roleplaying and of course video games. Tabletop roleplaying games (TTRPGs) are a continuation of that ancient act of sitting around a campfire and sharing stories. The popularity of TTRPGs probably grew out of the fact that people in modern societies started spending less and less time together under the same roof, families became smaller and people spread out into larger and larger cities. Sharing stories in a group became a rare occasion as people became less connected physically and culturally. Roleplaying filled that void to connect people around a shared story, creating a subculture of its own that everyone could participate in, regardless of their own origin. Video game RPGs allow you to always be the main character, the world revolves around you and you always get to be the hero. It's a pretty nice feeling that people crave over and over.

VISION QUESTS

Another anthropological aspect of video games is their audio-visual nature. As the name implies, we use video technology to create visions and worlds of countless variety. Ancient storytellers also used audio-visual elements to enhance their stories and games. Costumes, music, noise makers, fire, paint, sculpture, hallucinogens, etc. are all tools in the ancient storytellers' audio-visual repertoire. The modern game designer also uses audio-visual illusions to immerse the player in the story-game. This is a very ancient tradition stretching back to prehistory. In a manner of speaking, a game designer is not unlike the shaman guiding the player on a vision quest.

As an illustration of how powerful audio-visual storytelling is in human culture, the Chauvet Cave is a very clear example of how the way we told stories in the past is directly linked to how we tell them now with our modern technology. This ancient Palaeolithic cave was discovered in southern France in 1994. It remained untouched for approximately 25,000 years by a rock fall, preserving a plethora of ancient cave paintings depicting different species of animals as well as abstract shapes. Carbon dating suggests that the first humans to paint the walls did so around 37,000 years ago. What sets Chauvet apart from other similar Palaeolithic painted rock discoveries is the geology of the cave roof. The roof has a series of smooth stone bulges on which the animal art was painted, giving it an organic, almost 3D appearance (Figure 1.4). Instead of just being painted on flat surfaces, these animals were depicted using the contours of the stone to give them shape, and multiple repeating images of these animals were painted so as to give the impression of movement. In other words, if you held a light source up to view the pictures and moved the light slowly around the stone bulge, you would see each image appear as the light moved – possibly the first example of animation in human history. It is easy to imagine the shaman holding up a torch to the different animals and telling the audience how she can bring the animal spirit to

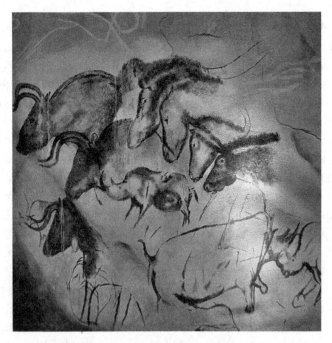

FIGURE 1.4 Galloping images, Chauvet Caves. (Courtesy of Wikimedia Commons.)

life as she slowly moved the angle of the light to make the animal painting spring to life. Using wind instruments and the acoustics of the cave to imitate the different calls of each species, the whole spectacle must have been impressive. This is explained in detail in the excellent documentary *Cave of Forgotten Dreams* by Werner Herzog. The most amazing element of the discovery was that evidence showed that the paintings had been retouched by generations for perhaps 3000 years of continuous use. In other words, people kept coming back to this cave for centuries to do audio-visual shows, retouching the paintings countless times.

Video games are just a modern extension of this very ancient and deep-seated social activity. As a game designer, you are tapping into this deeply rooted aspect of human culture and following an ancient tradition of entertaining others through games. It combines audio-visual storytelling with strategy and competition, all very ancient practices universal to all cultures. What a wonderful job to have!

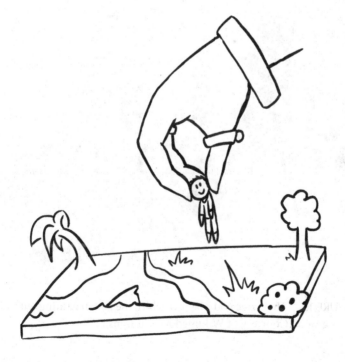

GAMES OF THE GODS

Several ancient cultures considered games to be reflections of the divine order of the universe. They represented a model of the hidden rules of probability and chance that seems to govern our lives but over which we have little control. In religious art around the world, gods are depicted gambling and playing board games (Figure 1.5). The gods of gaming are usually bringers of luck, tricksters who sometimes cheat their divine opponents in order to make gains for the human race. This personification of the elements of chance and the ups and downs of life is a very human way to explain the hidden forces that influence our life. Games are a way to reflect and use our imagination to see different possible futures for ourselves. They are mental models that take us through a process of meditation and thought when we play them, revealing complex truths about the world and life. The "collective unconscious", if you wish to

FIGURE 1.5   The Aztec god Macuilxochitl, the god of gaming with his RPG group. (Courtesy of Wikimedia Commons.)

use Jungian terminology, is visible in the games we have played and keep playing to the present.

One example from the medieval Europe is the Tarot (Figure 1.6). Based on playing cards that go back to 14th century Italy, this game became a method of divination and cartomancy with occult elements. Although not proven, some claim the symbolism of the cards borrows from medieval mysticism and many traditions including the Kabbalah, ancient Egypt, Indian Tantra, the I-Ching and others.

The interesting part to me about the Tarot is that they seem to reflect the base components of video games in card form.

FIGURE 1.6   Ready player zero, the fool card (le Mat), Tarot.

For example, there are four suits of 14 cards for a total of 56 Minor Arcana. The Minor Arcana to me mirror Bartle's Player Archetypes. The 22 "trump" cards, also called Major Arcana, each represent a mystical or philosophical concept, designed to help the readers reflect on their own life and possible choices. The Major Arcana, though originally supposed to represent the path of life, can also be used as a map of the player's journey through a video game. I will explain further along.

First a disclaimer: Not everyone believes in the validity of Bartle's model, and there has been much debate about its accuracy, relevance, etc. However, the basic premise of Bartle's system in my experience holds up to scrutiny. My contact with players and analysis of what drives their game preferences has led me to conclude that at the simplest level, there are in fact four basic player types. Though Bartle was perhaps focused on the psychology of players in massively multiplayer online games, he may have identified something that applies to all video game players. Or maybe he was describing something about human nature itself.

- **Achiever (Suit: Diamond, Tarot: Pentagram or Coins):** Describes players who like to gain the highest levels, best gear, rarest skins and get all the achievements. Game mechanics that please them: level systems, leader boards, ranks, rare loot, multiple currencies and unique skins that require a lot of effort. Achievers need an audience to tell them how great they are, and a forum by which their achievements can be compared to others. Bragging rights are important to achievers, and games should publish statistics and metrics to elevate the best players to public admiration.

- **Explorer (Suit: Clubs, Tarot: Wands):** This type of player wants to complete the game, explore every level, search every secret area, find the Easter eggs, even exploit the glitches and bugs that help them beat the game. They like to play each storyline to see all the possible endings, find the hidden ones and go back to their saved games to see how their choices would have played out differently. They are sometimes also called "completionists".

- **Socializer (Suit: Hearts, Tarot: Cups):** The majority of players fall into this category according to some research, though exactly how much is tough to guess. Socializers are the glue of player communities, sharing tips, participating in discussions and guilds, helping new players and engaging fellow players in group activities and joint efforts. Some of them end up being community leaders. This would suggest that socializers only play multiplayer games, but this is clearly not the case. Social elements are present in game narratives. Socializers are attracted to characters and story, and the game is secondary to their desire to see what happens next and how the story ends. Single-player games and even competitive games that include strong character design, interesting backstory and visual aesthetics can also appeal to socializers.

- **Killer (Suit: Spades, Tarot: Swords):** I personally believe that this archetype is much maligned and their name has obvious negative connotations. Killers are just achievers but of another sort, they enjoy the contest of defeating other players. They crave head-to-head contests and multiplayer fighting/combat. Killers find other players more challenging than AI and want everyone to know how good they are at playing against others.

What I find interesting about the parallel between the Tarot Minor Arcana and the player archetypes is that it points to a possible link between the two. I believe that medieval people, and people before them, were well aware of the different types of personalities in human psychology, before modern science formalized our understanding and language around it. Though not possessing the scientific data we now use, that never stopped people before from figuring out how the world works, and they probably expressed it through Jungian symbols and images rather than scientific terms. The Tarot and playing cards are an expression of that knowledge and point to a more general understanding of human nature. You could say that the Tarot is an expression of the Game of Life.

My point is I don't believe that the gamer archetypes are unique to gaming behaviour; I think they apply to human beings in general. If you strip out the gaming language, the four personality types are really not just gamer types, they are people types. Except of course, "Killers", who should be renamed as "Competitors" in my opinion since this is what they really enjoy doing. I think that all players have a "gamer personality" that closely matches their own non-gaming behaviour. Generally speaking, a person who is competitive in games is also competitive outside of games.

Basically, I believe that gaming behaviour does not exist only in the context of games, it is an expression of people's core personality. Games are just one way for people to express this preference, but you will find evidence that they do so in other mediums if you take the time to study their habits. If you could devise a test that could accurately rate everyone on the Bartle Spectrum, I am willing to bet that every player has a little bit of all four archetypes in their gamer DNA, they just strongly favour one over the others. What I mean is that all players have a bit of an achiever streak, explorer, socializer and competitor. In my case, for example, some games engage my achiever tendencies, some tickle my explorer side and others attract me for their strong sense of community or rich story, but I tend to gravitate towards competitive games.

Psychologically, everyone plays an inner game with themselves where they keep a secret score of their own life. Some people like to collect things, some people like to make many friends, some want the biggest house or the largest family, some like to travel, while others like to race cars. The point I am making is that everyone has a game they like to play, both in real life or in a video game. Video games simply tap into those personal games we play with ourselves in a more concentrated form, with direct stimulation of our strongest "winning" desires and without any real consequences of danger or failure. Video games are a harmless way to express these personal inner games that we keep track of and score ourselves on every day.

Ask any high achiever or collector or entertainer what drives them and if they think they are successful or a failure. Social media is just one way we like to keep score or compete with each other. How many people use it to post photos of their idyllic life or fantastic travel adventures? Others gather real physical trophies like cars, money or companies. Everyone plays games; some of us also play video games.

One interesting game from ancient India is the game of Leela. Over 2000 years old according to some scholars, the game was created to teach moral lessons and as a way to meditate on one's life and path to self-improvement. It was adapted in modern times into the game most people know as Snakes and Ladders, but the original game has deep spiritual traditions and uses the element of chance to illustrate personal learning opportunities. The guru guides the players through the meanings of the various events they encounter on the board as a form of Ludomancy, interpreting the possible meanings as a guide to each player's life journey.

These examples demonstrate that games go beyond simple entertainment and leisure. I believe every game has the power to create an inner reflective space, if you include elements that allow players to see their own experiences and aspirations mirrored inside. These are powerful storytelling tools that should not be neglected in your quest to create the most intense gaming experiences. Some games can take on aspects of spiritual meditation, and game creators build worlds that have lessons to teach and moral paths to choose from. Such games allow us to reflect on the world around us and understand the sometimes hidden rules that underpin its complexities.

CONCLUSION

Video games come from a deeply rooted human instinct to play games; cultures around the world have been engaged in gaming since before human civilization. Game designers are tapping into powerful individual and social instincts when they create gameplay that brings out our deeply rooted need to play, our desire to share stories and to understand the world we live in. If you keep in mind the psychological, cultural and social aspects of why people play when you design, you can create games that are more powerful experiences and greater than the sum of their parts.

CHAPTER 2

Game Designer Specializations

The role of game designers in video game development may seem obvious, but there is plenty of debate within the industry as to exactly what designers do and what they are responsible for. In the past, some companies did not believe in having a position called "designer", even today some famous studios do not have a position called "game designer". This is rare as most of the industry has accepted the need for designers, but there are some famous titles that were built by only programmers and artists. This is certainly possible; after all, everyone is a game designer.

What I mean is that everyone can come up with ideas for games, most people who play games can come up with mechanics or concepts for a game. But as most industry people know, ideas are easy, execution is the tough part. Game designers are not the smartest people with the smartest game ideas. That attitude will quickly get a designer into trouble; it is arrogant to presume that as a designer you are the source of the best game ideas. New designers are especially prone to this misconception, it is an honest mistake. Most healthy development teams use ideas from any source; anyone in the team should be able to express an idea and throw it into the discussion about game design, if the process is properly managed. The benefits of this approach are immense to the DNA of a game, as no one person is as smart as the collective inspiration of the entire team.

However, this does not mean that video game designers are less important, or that games should be designed by committee. The designer's role is to conceive and collect the best ideas, communicate them to the team in a sustained and consistent level, then shepherd those ideas through the development process until they come out as fully mature and polished game features. In other words, game design is much more than just coming up with smart ideas, it is also about editing and following through on them. This is much harder than it sounds, and it requires forethought, analytical skills, the ability to estimate and weight variables and unknowns, as well as to mitigate a whole ton of risk factors in a complex management and team environment. Sounds rather impossible when you express it in those terms, but it gets done every day by many talented people.

The game designer's role is not universally defined from studio to studio. There are many different kinds of designers, and they are becoming more specialized as the industry becomes larger and projects become more complex. If you are just starting out in this field, it may be helpful to understand the different types of designers so you can steer towards the job that best suits your temperament and personality. Keep in mind that the following job descriptions are not universal or standard, different studios load different responsibilities on each type of designer.

Unlike a programmer or an artist that has a well-defined set of technical skills and jobs to do, "game designer" is a catch-all term that encompasses a wide variety of roles and responsibilities. It also varies widely from platform to platform. My primary focus here is on console and personal computer (PC) development design. In the field of virtual reality (VR) or mobile development, designers take on different jobs and perform tasks that are unique to their technology and platform, so don't take this list as absolute. You may want to think about what kind of designer suits your skills, inborne talent and passion as you set out on your development career. If you want to become "that kind" of designer, focus on the type of projects and skills that will get you there.

Here are some of the types of specialist design roles in the industry.

TECH DESIGNER

This type of designer has a programming background and other technical skills. Depending on the robustness of the engine tools, they may be necessary in assisting design teams manipulate game data, updating server information for live content games and helping create game builds in large complex

projects. They have an interest in game design, along with strong technical skills that allow them to manipulate engine data and create gameplay content independently of code support. Some programming teams use a tech designer to interface between their team and the design team, or the design team has a tech designer to implement more technical gameplay changes without requiring programming support. Note that this role is different from a gameplay programmer, who is a special type of programmer that works on game-design-related tasks and gameplay coding.

CHARACTER DESIGNER

Usually an artist by trade, this type of designer specializes in creating both player and non-player characters (NPCs). The job may include the concept art, animation design, character backstory, voice and the specific gameplay of the character. This type

of designer is more common in heavily character-driven games like brawlers, multiplayer online battle arena (MOBA) and multiplayer player versus player (pvp) titles to name a few. They specialize in making characters memorable, designing personality and recognizable behaviours that players find appealing and elegant.

INTERFACE DESIGNER

Another art related discipline, user interface (UI) design is a critical skill for games. This type of designer may have 2D art skills and can create assets for programmers to integrate into the UI system. They design the layout and functionality of the UI, down to the colours, animations and the logic flow. An important part of the job is to make the UI consistent, visually appealing and logical. The player should have all the information needed to play the game without the UI elements interfering with the other visual aspects of the game, a tricky balancing act.

MENU DESIGNER

A specialty skill, this type of UI designer deals with complex menu systems. Some games have heavy menu interaction in between segments of play. Multiplayer games also tend to have heavier demands on menu flow for matchmaking, gameplay selection and management (consumables, unlocking progression, etc.). This skill not only involves designing menu flow and logic, but needs a good eye for esthetics and placement of interactive elements to keep the game flowing and the information easy to find and read.

SYSTEM DESIGNER

Most games have system designers, even if they are not referred to by that title. These designers create gameplay systems and features, such as progression systems, crafting mechanics, combat gameplay, etc. Sometimes this means creating a weapon, a playable car, a cover system, etc. The system designer usually carries the feature from concept to prototyping, to Alpha and Beta version. They are usually matched with a small team consisting of a programmer and an artist who are dedicated to the feature being designed. System designers are supposed to create their own features, sell them to the team and then shepherd their systems all the way to the finish line. They must be analytical as well as capable of organizing the team around their development needs and be able to negotiate and sell their ideas. They must be passionate enough to be the champion for their features, while at the same time pragmatic enough to critically analyse their own work.

ARTIFICIAL INTELLIGENCE (AI) DESIGNER

Increasingly games have a heavier reliance on complex AI behaviour or on a large number of different behaviours. When there are a lot of complex interactions and a wide range of AI types, teams may give the job to a specialized AI designer. Specialists in AI design work closely with the programming and art team to define requirements and behaviours. They map out the total

"population" and communicate with the level design team on how best to utilize and distribute the various types of AI opponents. In some cases, AI is designed to assist the player as NPCs, and they have to be crafted carefully to be useful while not stealing the player's thunder. Sometimes AI is not about a group of opponents but a background process that operates various feedbacks and event mechanisms that drive the core game experience. There are many examples of games that rely heavily on the inner process of AI as its core gameplay mechanism to drive moment to moment and the meta loop.

BOSSFIGHT DESIGNER

Tuning bossfights is challenging and requires a lot of experience and time to iterate properly. Sometimes considered a specialized AI designer, this role becomes important in games where the bossfights are numerous and central features of the game. Bossfights in themselves are large complex features. Each bossfight usually requires a custom environment, elaborate modelling

and animations, as well as unique effects and gameplay systems. A mini game unto themselves in some cases, they take a lot of time to craft and polish, so these specialized type of designers are becoming more common on larger projects.

COMBAT DESIGNER

This type of designer is dedicated to crafting combat for all kinds of genres. More commonly seen on brawlers or action games, combat designers not only outline the total scope of the combat system but detail each weapon, move, power, spell and define how it all works together into a seamless and fun experience. This role may sometimes include AI design, sometimes bossfights or even level design, depending on the project. Some combat designers specialize in a genre, such as fighting games, while others are more on the simulation or strategy side of things like real-time strategies. Combat designers are also experts in balancing, they can tweak to perfection each weapon, ability or player skill so as not to favour one style or leave the system

open to exploits. They are usually proficient in mathematics and statistics, random number generation systems and comparative analysis techniques.

BALANCE DESIGNER

In game projects where there are multiple interlocking systems and a large range of features, deep progression and multiple live release scheduled, it is difficult for a design team to retain detailed knowledge of the entire game feature set. Design teams can become completely overwhelmed by the sheer scope of a game and

they must dedicate one designer to maintaining a living knowledge of the balance scheme for the entire game. Massively multiplayer online games (MMOs) are especially prone to become too big for each designer to do their own balancing inside their own feature set. Balance designers are also sometimes used in the latter stages of game production to bring an independent objective eye in the polishing and closing phase. In games that have live content and frequent patches, the balance designer compares each new fix, change or feature against the overall system and the established metas to make sure that the overall integrity of the game systems are preserved. Balance designers often rely on community input and independent testing to assess balancing needs.

ECONOMY DESIGNER

A specialist that sometimes has a degree or some kind of training in economics, their job is to create a working game economy and maintain its ongoing health in the face of new features and constant player attempts to manipulate it. Economy design can be the most important feature of certain classes of games, in particular, free to play (F2P) titles and MMOs. This person relies on a deep knowledge of how online market places work, mathematics, statistics analysis and financial models. Their responsibilities can include creating storefront menus, resource gathering

gameplay systems, marketplace design, loot systems, player auction houses and live price adjustment using various analytical tools. Designing an economy on paper and then releasing it to a live community are two different skills and sometimes a different designer is assigned to each phase.

USER EXPERIENCE DESIGNER

This is a specialist versed in ergonomics, visual language and usability markers. They sometimes have a background in psychology or visual design, and can be former UI or menu artists. Some games require this specialist due to the sheer amount of menus, mini games or UI modes that require a unified standard and visual signature. This is a growing branch of design in VR, which has special requirements in this area due to the physical and psychological demands these games put on players.

LEVEL DESIGNER

A more common design job, level designers specialize in creating worlds and environments where the gameplay elements are used. They are sometimes versed in architecture theory or art. They study interesting environments, learn what makes them

interesting to traverse and try to apply them to game spaces. Depending on the complexity of the technology, they can be involved in the concepting, greyboxing and dressing of the levels. They often work with a dedicated environment artist or designer to make their levels visually consistent and interesting. They try to tell a story in their layouts, through the placement of enemies, obstacles and rewards. They are versed in critical pathing, save points and visual language. Level designers are often more in number than game designers on a team as console projects become bigger and bigger. They operate to tight deadlines and they have to be organized and methodical.

ENVIRONMENT DESIGNER

Environment designers are not level designers, but related. They specialize in dressing detailed environment with art assets that help bring the levels to life, and make the look authentic and pleasing. They often come from the art side and have a decorator's sense both in terms of interior design and landscaping. This type of designer is usually associated with projects with detailed 3D environments and open-world games where large levels need to have specific areas dressed up for story or visual signage. They may also be involved in the initial concept phase for levels, helping with lighting, set design and asset creation.

STORY/NARRATIVE DESIGNER

These are the writers specialized in gameplay dialog and systems for interacting with NPCs, they come from a professional writing background or a cinematics/dialog background. They are often involved in the design of the dialog system, NPCs and AI interactions. They sometimes script and produce cut scenes, in-game

cinematic sequences or background material that is presented in game depending on the genre. Story designers will often have input on environment and level design so that they support story settings and locations.

QUEST DESIGNER

Similar to story designers, these types of designers are common in MMOs and open-world games that rely on a huge number of quests to support a long-term player base ever hungry for content. They are usually responsible for creating the entire quest dialog, the flow of the quest, branching, descriptions, scripts and loot/rewards. They are often involved in creating enemy populations, NPCs and triggers for quest stages, depending on the tools being used. Some games have hundreds of quests that require large quest designer teams constantly working to update and create new content. Live game quest design is another skill set that requires good knowledge of community preferences, user statistics and the functioning of the game

economy to tweak existing quests and keep them updated with new features and patches.

ENCOUNTER DESIGNER

Some games have hundreds of encounters with mixed AI types. When the job is too large for the level designers, they usually appoint someone to design encounters separately. Open-world games and MMOs often have this type of designer. They are expert in the AI behaviours of all NPCs and enemies. They know how to create random encounters as well as scripted ones, and they can use the balancing systems to script encounters to match player abilities. They are good at pacing encounters so as to create peaks and valleys of fun, and they can populate environments optimally with the right kind of encounters at the right pace.

SCRIPTING DESIGNER

Some projects require designers that are specialized in scripting tools; usually this type of designer has a technical background with a designer's flair. Games that rely on heavily scripted cinematics, encounters, quests, events, AI behaviour, etc. use script designers to create game-related technical content, while

programmers focus on engine code and builds. Some studios consider scripting to be the main job of game designers, while others consider scripting a subset of gameplay programming. The need for script designers really depends on the type of game and the engine technology being used.

PRODUCTION DESIGNER

Some studios combine the role of producer with the designer role. The exact responsibilities vary with each studio but generally speaking, a production designer specializes in allocating resources to develop features created by the design team. They have the power of a producer while at the same time making judgement calls on whether the cost to make certain gameplay features is worth the resources required. Some lead designers do this as part of their job, some teams allocate this to a specialized production designer who is independent of the lead designer but not a pure producer (who are not supposed to make creative decisions). This role really depends on how the studio organizes hierarchies and responsibilities between production and design.

CREATIVE DIRECTOR

Some designers eventually migrate to the creative director job, but there are cases where this role is filled by someone outside of the design discipline, such as an art lead or programmer. Designers who wish to be creative directors must have good soft skills, the ability to speak in public and communicate effectively both in person and in writing. In addition to having good design

instincts and a very good understanding of gamer audiences, they should be knowledgeable in current market trends. They possess the ability to communicate complex design ideas to different audiences, from juniors to publishing and studio management. Lead designers who move into creative direction have to let go of some of the direct hands-on involvement they are accustomed to in design; creative directors write vision documents and present ideas, they don't generally detail game systems or feature mechanics. For this reason, some lead designers do not wish to move into this less hands-on role.

DESIGN DIRECTOR

Usually the head of the design department, a lead designer may eventually migrate to this role depending on the size of the studio and the number or size of projects. This person has strong managerial and lots of project experience, especially leading

design and designers. The design director ensures that the design department is running properly and the designs coming out of it are meeting a quality standard, both in terms of the game's needs and how well the design team is working with the other teams. The design director is supposed to make important calls when scope or schedule issues crop up, they are not supposed to do the day-to-day design work but instead supervise the lead designers and lead level designers. An important operational role, they are different from creative directors in that they have managerial responsibility for the department of design and possibly multiple game projects under the same studio.

PRINCIPAL DESIGNER

Some studios like to differentiate between managerial designers and designers with senior experience but no interest or inclination for management. The principle designer can lead documentation and is responsible for the quality of gameplay, but does not have direct responsibilities for hiring or firing, discipline or managerial duties within the design department.

DESIGN MANAGER

A pure management position, at the other end of the scale of the principle designer, these are experienced designers who are given supervisory tasks over the design department. Usually they come from a management background or have a strong affinity for leading departments in a supervisory capacity. They do little actual design work if any; they instead directly manage all designers in the studio. They interview/hire designers for all projects, they track their performance and manage their careers. They solve leadership issues, work with production to place the best people with the best projects and are responsible for the morale and effectiveness of the design department.

CHAPTER 3

Game Design Leadership

This section is not about game design techniques – that subject is so broad and personal to each designer that a chapter would barely scratch the surface. In addition, my fun is not your fun; everyone likes different things and as a good designer, you should be true to yourself. Trying to make someone else's idea (or "formula") of fun is rarely successful. I guess that, in itself, is my advice on game design technique: do what you know, follow your instincts.

The main point of this chapter is how to be an effective design leader in a development team. This is just a catalog of my personal observations over the years. It is neither a definitive pronouncement on the subject nor a standard that everyone should try to reach; it's just a collection of personal lessons learned over the years. Take them or leave them in whole or in part, ignore them, share them – do as you will.

I have never really considered design itself difficult. What I mean is, coming up with gameplay ideas or concepts for a game has been the fun part – the easy part, I guess. What has been the difficult part of learning my trade is how to work in a development team, and specifically work with the different disciplines in development.

As a designer, you don't work in a vacuum. Everything you do affects other people's work in the team, and learning to understand that effect and how to be a professional is the key to successful design implementation. The following is a collection of conclusions on the subject after spending more than two decades in entertainment software industry.

Regardless of what kind of game you work on, design leadership is at the center of success or failure. Every studio has its own approach to managing design work, but these recommendations should apply in most cases.

EFFECTIVE GAME DESIGN

The key to being an effective designer is understanding that you are at the center of a workflow that affects all the other disciplines. Design decisions affect art, sound, technology, production plans, budget and marketing. Assuming you have good design instincts, fresh ideas and a creative capacity, the key to being successful as a design leader is first understanding the high profile that your work has in the team.

The first thing that should come to mind when you realize this is to have respect, or humility, as Kim Swift of "Portal" fame put it. You are in a tremendously powerful and sensitive position; you are going to have a major impact on the success of this project without necessarily having authority in the team hierarchy.

And even if you do have that authority, it should rarely, if ever, be used. Respect the other disciplines and their role in the project. They are not there to execute your ideas; you are going to work with them to create something fun, together. You work for them as much as they may work for you. Nothing turns off a team more than an arrogant and imposing designer who throws out his "vision" in vague public speeches or voluminous documents and expects them to turn into concrete gameplay.

Without the respect of the team, there will be resistance during development – even if not overt or obvious. A team that does not feel like partners in the design process will question design choices and direction, will remain pessimistic about gameplay decisions long after they have been implemented and generally negatively impacts the project. This kind of atmosphere can affect everything in the game; things will take longer to make, features that had potential will get cut because they go over budget and finally, the biggest downer: crunch is never far behind.

This is not to say that the designer is responsible for everything that can go wrong in a project, projects fail for many different reasons, but the central role of your work puts you in a position to affect the delicate relationships between all teams, so be mindful of this situation and always act with the intent of earning the team's respect and trust in a long term way. How do you earn the team's respect? Here are some suggestions:

Be prepared. Whenever you are meeting with other disciplines to discuss implementation, make sure you are prepared with the latest information, updated documents and a set of possible solutions from design. Developers don't like doing your job for you; if asked for information on how something is supposed to work, don't throw it back at them and ask them to figure it out.

Have an answer, or work something out based on information they provide.

If there is a decision to be made, understand the options and the consequences for each option and make precise choices. That means you should be an encyclopedia on the project and this is easier for you as the designer to achieve, because you have more contact with all the different disciplines. You are somewhat of a central repository for what everyone is doing, so use that position to share and communicate the current state of progress on the project. This leads to…

Make decisions. Artists/animators, engineers and sound designers work according to precise schedules and budgets. They must produce assets at a predictable rate and give regular constant updates on the progress of their work. Nothing can upset this more than failure to make design decisions when they are needed or making vague ones.

Designers have to provide concrete and hard information when discussing the asset requirements for features with the team. No design document will ever provide all the information necessary for these teams to work independently of your input. You must interpret the design for them, modify it if necessary due to the myriad technical or production related limits and provide a final say when it is necessary to have that precision.

If you need to make a decision on the spot, make it, record it (by email) and stick to it. Nobody expects you to be right all the time or even to have all the answers, but they do expect you to make design decisions. When you fail to do this, you introduce uncertainty and leave things up in the air. It's better to risk making a mistake than to not make a decision at all. And you will make wrong decisions; all designers do. Which leads us to…

Don't worry about being wrong. Some things that you thought were fun and cool won't be in the final cut, and that is part of development. Don't worry about some of your ideas not working out in the end; worry about the game as a whole. Some of your ideas will fail for reasons that do not invalidate the idea itself.

It could be due to scoping issues, or a technical issue no longer making it feasible, another feature rendering it obsolete… Don't sweat about your precious idea getting rejected after playtesting; games are created in an iterative process, and you can only find out if something is really going to work once it is actually prototyped. Until then, it is just theory, based on your design instincts. Speaking of theory…

Don't let the document do the talking for you. The game design document is not a blueprint for making an awesome game. It is a set of theoretical choices on gameplay, with a theoretical fun final objective. It will change a lot during development and new information will modify its content rapidly.

That doesn't mean there is no point in writing one; even if it gets changed often, you still need to start somewhere, and the first versions of the design document are critical to shaping the overall vision and strategy of the project. However, many people will interpret it differently – one sentence will mean something totally different to another team member. Engineers may need more information to understand something that is perfectly clear to an animator.

The design document is the starting point of your collaboration with the rest of the team; it is not the final result of your work. Make sure that when you put out a design document for the team, you go over it with the relevant department leads and people working on that feature. Yes, this means that you must schedule a meeting before they start working and go over the whole thing in detail.

It really helps if everyone at this meeting has read it beforehand. During the meeting you will get a flurry of questions about stuff that you thought was perfectly clear in the document; this is normal and, in fact, healthy!

It means that you were not precise enough for certain people or that there was an ingrained assumption about the feature inherited from previous discussions. This is what this meeting is designed to iron out, and get everyone on the same understanding about what exactly this design is trying to achieve.

It also allows you to solicit input from the implementation group on how to execute features. The meeting should result in clarifications and small changes to the document, and you should integrate those changes as quickly as possible and update the feature document for the participants to review as quickly as possible after the meeting – memories fade fast.

That process turns the document from a draft to a Version 1, and you are now off to the races. Talking through the document will save you enormous pain down the line, and gives the team members the chance to shape the design and inject their own ideas. You want this to happen – trust me. The best games come from this collaboration. You must be confident enough as a designer to...

THE IMPORTANCE OF FEEDBACK

Ask for opinions and take other people's ideas on board. Be open and willing to acknowledge better ideas from others on the team, especially ideas outside the design group. This does not mean design by committee, nor should you hold a massive brainstorming session with the entire team – this will just result in a mess and make you seem uncertain and indecisive.

You are the designer; you are being paid to design the game. It is your responsibility, but all the ideas do not have to come from you; in fact, the best games are the combination of all the best ideas from the entire team. If you manage this process properly, whereby you can keep the design coherent yet at the same time adapt good ideas from others into it, you will have much better game DNA.

If your process is insular and exclusive of outside input, you will end up with an inbred design. It may look healthy and whole until released into the wild; then its crippling flaws will become obvious. At the other extreme, if design decisions are made by a committee, you end up with a Frankenstein game that is basically everyone's favorite personal feature from their favorite game forcefully stitched together in a painful and unnatural way. It never works.

Managing that middle ground takes confidence and experience, but if you are designing what you know (as opposed to someone else's idea of fun), it will be easier to navigate this tightrope. And it is a tightrope, because opening the floor to design ideas can be tricky if you are not confident enough about your design from the start.

If you understand what you are trying to achieve, then you will quickly be able to earn the confidence of the team by explaining your decisions and making them see why you made those choices. Remember that people outside of the design team don't spend all their time thinking about design issues, and so they don't have the big picture that you are supposed to have as the designer. It's easy for them to look at a single feature and come up with a "better" idea outside of the context of the entire game system. This kind of second guessing may feel distracting and a challenge to your decisions, but don't make the mistake of ignoring these kinds of questions.

This is an opportunity for you, not a challenge to your ideas. This is where you start giving them a hint at how complex and interwoven the gameplay big picture is, and how much you have a grip on understanding it. It is okay to not have the answer to all the questions that come up during development, but you should have a few scenarios, or options, in mind. By walking your colleagues through your thought process, you demonstrate that you have considered multiple approaches even if you are still not completely certain about the final outcome.

This process should be informal. People should feel free to mention ideas to the design team at any time, without any expectations either way. Make them understand that you are comfortable listening to ideas and that you won't consider such a thing a challenge to your work. Be open and friendly about sharing the design and your job will be much easier. To manage that process well you need to...

THE IMPORTANCE OF OBJECTIVITY

Be objective about your own ideas. Just because you are the designer doesn't mean that you are going to have all the best ideas for the game. You will need a lot of help, and if you shut out others from being part of that process, you will lose a massive resource: the accumulated brainpower of the entire team! In order to cultivate that collaborative relationship with the team,

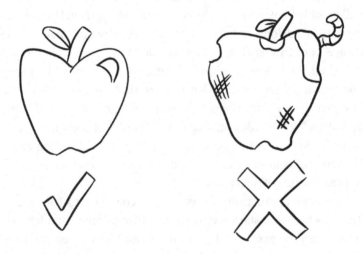

you have to learn to tame your own ego. You must be honest about your ideas and those of others.

It's easy to get defensive, as a designer, when you have all the experience and the job title but someone from an unrelated department comes up with something that is frankly better than what you had chosen. You have to be able to honestly admit to yourself first that this is a good idea, and then vocalize it to the rest of the team if you think it fits with the overall game.

It's not going to make them lose respect for you; on the contrary, it will increase their trust in your decisions when they can see that you are being objective and leaving your ego at the door. Vocalizing it also important – publicly acknowledging the merits and source of the idea is very important to earning the respect of the team.

If you take someone else's idea and secretly stick it into the design, you will have earned nothing but contempt on two levels, first because you don't have the honesty to admit when you are wrong, and second because you are taking credit for someone else's idea. Even if it's not true and you had no intention of doing either, nothing will tank you reputation with the team faster.

Being able to honestly evaluate the merits of a design idea regardless of authorship is key to being a good designer; there is no way in hell you will ever be able to make 100 percent of the design decisions 100 percent correctly, so listen to the team! Objectivity is also important to the people who pay for all of this.

THE BUSINESS SIDE

Respect the business. Game development can be complex because of the uneasy mix of business and entertainment. In some entertainment industries, this marriage is well managed due to decades of experience honing that relationship. Yet there are still spectacular failures in the movie industry, despite over a century of refinement.

Things will not change in game development any time soon either. Technology is one factor; changes in the business model and evolving tastes are others. The end result is that it's easy to unbalance the relationship between the business and game side of the things.

One way that you, as a design leader, can help maintain that balance is to understand the factors that are at the foundation of your project: the business conditions. This is one of the most important skills you will need to be an effective leader in design. This doesn't mean that you need to get inside the numbers that management deals with; it just means that you should know the lay of land – the strategy behind your project.

A good tactician understands what the prevailing conditions are at the strategic and logistical level. In development terms, you should be designing within the budget, within the technology scope and to the projected release plan. This is tricky; I have seen some designers become more a part of the marketing team than the development team as a result of being too preoccupied with the sales strategy side of the job.

Don't try to do upper management's job, but at the same time, be aware of their plan and expectations on budget and sales and let them know you understand it. They need to know you are objective as well as passionate. This really comes down to the fact that your features should fit the scope, whether it's a $500,000, $5 million or $50 million game.

WORKING WITH OTHER DISCIPLINES

Each discipline in game development has its own "Culture", and as a designer, you need to learn how to speak their language, see development from their point of view and understand their workflows and challenges. Not only will this build trust and professional respect, but will also allow you to design better features knowing how these other disciplines implement your work. It gives you a better understanding on how to negotiate your features with them and adapt your design to the technical and production restrictions each discipline controls.

Working with Programmers

Programmers work in very precise and concrete terms. Whatever feature you have come up with, they will have to make it happen down to the smallest detail and in doing so, they will be carrying the design mantle that you hand off once you have outlined the feature.

Be precise when discussing implementation with programmers. Mathematical formulas are nice, if you can provide them. Provide feature lists with all asset requirements, exact details on mechanics and systems. Point form information is best for this kind of documentation. Programmers don't like sifting through paragraphs of flowery language, backstory details and character bios when looking for the information they need to code. Provide functional diagrams, failure and edge cases, alternative implementation options, plan B versions – as much as they ask for or need.

Some programming teams want to get directly into the design with you. Great! Build a mutual understanding of the gameplay objectives together, then discuss nuts and bolts as they require. Be available to the engineering leads to work on stuff according to their needs. Don't just begin publishing documents as the mood strikes you; ask the programming leads to give you a work list that will satisfy their information needs according to their pipeline. If you can be Johnny-on-the-Spot with the information they need when they need it, you will be working together and properly aligned.

Programmers need to know that the information that you are providing is relevant to their current work; they don't want to sift through a large bunch of documentation looking for the information they need. Direct your documentation to their needs and at the level of detail they need, when they need it. If you cannot detail a feature because of a dependency on something else, then discuss the dependency and agree to a mutual plan of action.

This essentially means that you should be writing two levels of documentation: big-picture-level stuff that gives overall vision and scoping detail for general team consumption, and nuts-and-bolts-design documents that are as direct and precise as possible regarding features and mechanics. Engineering leads may have a preference for the format and style of this kind of documentation; talk to them and find out what would suit them best.

Working with Artists

Artists, modelers, and animators deal in aesthetics as well as concrete asset production. The important part for you as a designer is to not intrude upon their area of expertise – the aesthetics, or simply put, the art.

When reviewing art assets or discussing art direction, don't become an artist. Make sure you keep your designer hat on and leave the art to the artists. If they solicit your input on an aesthetic call, give your personal preference by all means – but know that nothing turns off artists more than a wannabe art critic. If you have artistic training, great, make sure that they know you may have some basis for your opinion, but don't try to be the art director as well as the creative one.

If you want artists to be part of the design process, ask them for options and preferences and see if that works or fits the game. You want to cultivate their artistic sensibility so that they pour their best work into the game. If you criticize art choices based on personal preferences rather than what is objectively best for the game, then you shut them down as partners in the process.

When you ask for art assets, make sure that you get into stylistic dos and don'ts before they start working on them. Telling an artist that your game is not steampunk style after they made a character model is never going to win you points. Be clear about what the game is NOT about as well as what it is stylistically close to.

Some art teams want precise, detailed designs on all art-related components; some teams want to be able to interpret the art needs from the design direction. Make sure you work with the style they prefer. If it is detailed they want, then detailed you give. If they prefer to be left to make assets according to their interpretation, then try to work with that and harness their creative talent while of course keeping it within the scope of the design.

Animators merit a special mention. This is a crucial relationship depending on how much animation your game uses. Animations have a huge impact on performance and the final appearance and polish level. It is easy to become overzealous in animation and break the memory bank, but if you go too cheap, your game will not compete visually; finding that fine balance requires a close understanding between you and the animation team.

What is the minimum that your design can live with, and what is the "would-be-awesome" extra that would really give you more bang for the buck is a tough thing to work out ahead of time. Working closely with animation throughout the project is important to maintain that balance. Keep on top of animation design, make sure that the designers and animators are in agreement and provide precise lists of requirements as the animation team needs. Make sure that the animators and gameplay designers are both working on the same page in terms of visual bang for asset buck.

Working with Sound Designers

Sound is psychologically a huge part of the game experience (right up there with the visuals). I go online and look for soundtracks of games that I played almost 20 years ago because they bring such a rush of nostalgia and good memories. There is something very primordial about sound, as far as its role in building the emotional experience.

Your relationship to your sound design team should be such that you both understand what kind of mood you want to build in the game. You should review the design with them and ask them to pitch you music and sound effects that would match it. It's just like scoring a film, and just as important.

The best way to show them what you mean is videos and sound files. Once you agree on the atmosphere you want to create, the rest should be relatively smooth. If you are providing dialog for them, or even directing recording sessions, make sure that you are open to changing things on the fly. Experienced sound people know what sounds right; don't be resistant to changing your script based on the sound designer's or voice actor's different interpretation of it. Something that looks good on paper may be totally silly out loud. Just like the other disciplines, be willing

to make your material better with the creative input of those who have the experience to know.

Working with Production

The production team is in a delicate position between the development team and upper management. Answering to both can be tricky and may lead to a lot of stress.

A good production team should consider itself more a part of the development team than a voice of upper management. You, as the designer, can help make them feel part of the team by including them in your design reviews, implementation meetings and even some of your design team discussions. This may make you nervous of producers interfering in the design process, but good producers don't consider themselves designers and leave the designing to the people responsible for it.

The more they know, the better they will be able to help you. Keeping them in the loop gives them the information they need to feel on top of things. A good way to do this is regularly record major implementation meetings in note form and publish them to production in emails, if they can't have a production member present at each such meeting. In this way, they will be able to represent the team's goals and direction to upper management in a transparent manner in terms that are more relevant to that level of leadership.

When an upper manager can see more clearly what is happening on the shop floor, they put less pressure on production, which then flows down to the team. Producers are your boss, but in a more collaborative way than just purely subordinate-manager relationship. The producer is your ally; they will settle disputes between teams, mediate, make final calls and drive things forward when they need to.

A good producer knows that all creative collaborations are full of differences in opinion and methodology; they avoid becoming a conduit for these tensions, instead keeping the politics and rivalries to a minimum, making calls for the good of the project and quashing the rumor mill.

To illustrate what makes a good producer, let me use a film industry anecdote:

Famous actor Michael Caine shared a personal experience in a televised interview. While he was filming *Zulu*, the movie that made him a star, he was quite nervous as a young actor, and was not quite sure how to play the part of a military officer. He decided that to appear to have more authority, he should keep his hands clasped behind his back during his scenes.

It wasn't long before he began hearing rumors that another actor was complaining about his performance, that he didn't know what to do with his hands. Caine became nervous and went to the producer, worried that he was about to get fired. When he asked the producer about the complaints, the reply was (and I paraphrase in this more polite version) Well, you haven't heard anything about it from me, have you? Now get on with it. Knowing the producer was on top of the things that gave him the confidence to pour his energies into his acting and enabled him to give the performance of a lifetime.

Working with Writers

People who write game dialog and text have the challenge to produce a lot of material for a fast changing set of content that may or may not be drastically changed or cut during production. They have to wait until major gameplay systems, environments and story are finished before they can start to implement the final text, record the voice sessions and start work on localized versions. They have to adapt old material or replace it on the fly and maintain the overall consistency of terms, characters, etc. It's a challenging job with its own technical and production constraints. It is very important to keep writers updated with the very latest design decisions and content maps. Working closely with them will ensure that they can adapt quickly and with minimum effort, which prevents you from making costly production decisions that end up requiring re-recordings, re-writes and cuts.

Writers require a lot of freedom to make their own impact and bring their own style. It's the only way they can focus on the large volume of content they need to produce usually in a short space of time. Aligning yourself with the writers early is very important because neither of you will have much time to check with each other as the production process goes into its final stages. Don't be precious about the names of character, plot points or other minor story elements that don't really affect the final game but help make the narrative content more elegant and streamlined. Just like sound designers can help make the game sound better, writers know what works better narratively and need to be given the leeway to bring that expertise into design decisions. Even better, adapt the design to their needs if you can, sometimes design can be a constraint to good story, a little flexibility can pay off.

Working with Marketing

The marketing team's relationship with design depends entirely on the company. Some studios like to integrate a person from marketing within the development team, some like to have marketing

involved from the very early stages of pitching and preproduction, while some only bring them in later closer to the shipping date. Your relationship with marketing is very important; it can make the difference in terms of an effective campaign that truly captures the qualities of the title you have been working on.

Good marketing teams are armed with lots of data and metrics, information about the competition and good social media skills. They can give you vital information and clues as to what to expect from the market landscape, and how you should respond to shifting tastes and strong competition. They may request materials from the game, quotes from you or the team, images, etc. to support their campaign. Some developers consider these requests a drain on resources, especially if the project is in overdrive and there are many tasks yet to finish. However, it is worthwhile supporting marketing requests, even tools for taking screenshots, videos, etc. that will give them the material they need to mount an effective promotion of your game.

Trust me, it is hard to sell games and even the most polished, fun and big name titles struggle to find audiences that are constantly bombarded with new releases. The process of matching an audience with a product is called "Discovery" and it's a very apt term, because it literally is almost like looking for gold in the hills. Sometimes you discover a gold mine, most of the time you keep searching.

Once you have finished or nearly finished the game, its fate rests in the hands of marketing. Your hard work will also play a part, of course, players will respond to good quality original game experiences, but first you need to find that audience and marketing is your critical partner in this final piece of the puzzle.

Working with Other Designers

Working with other designers can be the hardest part of the job. Why? It's simple: designers are an opinionated bunch. They have such strong opinions that they feel compelled to turn them into games. They have opinions about all kinds of things and turning

opinion into reality with a bunch of other opinionated know-it-alls can be quite tricky! Remind yourself that they are just as passionate as you are, and for the same love of games that you have. You are in this together.

Fun is a very personal thing. My fun is not necessarily your fun and vice versa. You will not share the same passion for different kinds of game fun, so try to find the areas where you have commonality and build that game. It is important not to seem to look down on other people's fun when discussing design.

Whatever your personal feelings, don't make it personal. That means you will have to change and adapt as much as everyone else. If you really absolutely feel very strongly about a particular element of gameplay, then by all means argue it, pitch it and sell it. But there is a big professional difference between fun and fanboy. Don't be a fanboy in design meetings. Stay passionate but be objective (I know I keep repeating this, but it is worth emphasizing.)

Don't shut down ideas because they are not your cup of tea; as always, remain objective and argue from the point of view of what is best for the overall game experience. And yes, you will have to argue – not in the negative sense, but in a "lawyer-making-a-case" sense. You should be able to explain the merits of your choices and decisions, test them against the opinions of the other designers and validate them as a group. Experienced designers don't get bogged down in arguments on what colour the character's hat should be; they fight the important battles and they argue rationally based on what is best for the game.

After the argument phase of design discussions, then comes the decision phase. If the group can agree on a course of action, great! If not, the design leader must make a call and move on. Either way, once the choice is made, do not keep picking away at it, and make sure everyone works to support the decision whether they initially agreed with it or not. Sometimes a designer is expected to come up with the idea, and sometimes they must follow someone else's. Make sure that everyone knows when the time for debate is over, and when the time to make it happen starts.

A little bit of creative tension is important for a healthy design team, but managing that is tricky. It is important to establish a clear design vision so that everyone is on the same page before discussing specific choices. You, as the design leader, must ensure you have provided that top-level framework that everyone's ideas should be directed to. Don't just start your design discussions with "we are going to make a painting", start with "we are going to paint a pastoral scene in the Romantic style. What should we put in it?" You also have to drive the design forward and make the final decisions if consensus cannot be achieved.

Another thing that is important to manage is consistency. Make sure you are saying the same thing to everyone and so is your design team. Don't get in a situation where your designers are contradicting each other in front of the other departments; it will just make you look like clowns and confuse the team. If the design team is not on the same page, you might be spending too much time meeting with the rest of the team than your designers.

Drive consensus and mutual agreement on features before you break out to work with the other teams. Designers can argue and debate in design meetings, not in implementation meetings. If you need to make a call, make sure you don't contradict that call later on. Nobody likes to throw work out. If you contradict your-self in the documentation, are vague or don't give proper expla-nations for what you expect as an end result, the consequence is lost work and grumpy developers.

Once you have everyone working away on features and devel-opment is chugging along, be sure to check on your designers outside of the regular Scrum meetings, group updates, etc. Some designers end up "going native" when they work too long embed-ded in a cross-functional team. Some of this is okay and to be expected. You want them to bond and feel ownership, but keep the central design team meetings alive, remind all the design-ers they serve the greater game interest – they don't belong to a feature "tribe".

Last piece of advice: if you are going to give a designer a spe-cific feature or design task, let them do it according to their game instincts. Assuming your direction has been clear, don't backseat drive a design; if you are going to hand it off, let them make the decisions and then evaluate the end result. If you give them a task and they need your permission to make choices, you are not really giving them the task at all, you are just setting them up to fail.

CONCLUSION

Game design may offer the most freedom and creativity but it comes with great responsibility. It is easy for a designer to come across as insensitive to the workflow of other departments or working outside of the group effort if they lose contact with the various teams. As you become immersed in the process of creat-ing a game, do not lose sight of the thoughts, needs and feelings of the team that you are building the game with. A large dose of diplomacy, psychology and professional self-discipline will go a long way to earn the trust and respect of the team, essential ingredients for great games.

CHAPTER 4

The Role of Communication

The most difficult aspect of video game project management is communication. This is especially a challenge for games as opposed to regular software development because it is difficult to accurately define in a simple and brief manner the totality of a game's features set verbally, and design documents become too cumbersome and time consuming to read over and over again in the pursuit of day-to-day tasks. This is made more demanding because every game is different and interpretations vary on the definition of each feature-set from person to person. Everyone on a team has their own personal set of game references they bring to the job, based on their own video game tastes and development experience; this means that the job of building consensus and mutual understanding of definitions and terms is a constant struggle for the design leader. In addition, as the project becomes larger and more people join the team during the production cycle, newcomers must be on-boarded quickly in order to contribute to the work, and this usually means they are not able to spend much time absorbing all the details of the design before they start contributing. Oftentimes, they are creating critical assets and features without the full context of how their work fits into the final version of the game.

In an ideal world, each person working on a game would have the time to learn about every aspect of the design, even those not directly related to their day-to-day tasks, but the costs of game development precludes this and even the design team itself is not able to fully absorb the complete game design as it grows into its final release version. To illustrate how massive games can become, oftentimes developers discover things they themselves did not know about games they have released until the player base has posted the information on public forums and wikis maintained by fans. In fact, I have worked in teams where it was often faster to look up fan-created sources rather than internal documents to quickly reference information such as gameplay data, stats or in-game terminology. A team of a hundred developers does not know as much about the game they made as a fan base of several thousand deconstructing every detail of the title and posting it online.

This is also the reason why a small team of developers can sometimes create much more innovative gameplay than large AAA teams. A small team of 6 people is able to communicate much more effectively on a day-to-day basis about the design than 50 or 1000 people distributed around the world. (So far a 1000 is the largest team size I have heard of, and 400–600 is not uncommon).

This is why the game industry has seen some spectacularly massive successes from small indie developers who have identified gameplay opportunities and were able to deliver boutique games to their fan base in ways that larger more cumbersome teams could not wrap their collective heads around. But let us not conclude that small teams are better at making games, on the contrary, there have been many uncounted failures that go unnoticed in indie development, the job of successful development is never easy no matter the size of the team and small teams have to deal with their own challenges, however, communication is usually not one of them. That does not mean this chapter does not apply to them.

Despite the impact communication issues can have, it tends to be underestimated in development planning. We assume that people will communicate automatically as part of their day-to-day work, but this is a false sense of security that a lot of teams sleepwalk into. The primary role of designers is to communicate ideas and information to different levels of the team and in different formats, making this job one of the trickiest balancing acts in game development. Communication has many different methods and styles, and it is possible to undercommunicate as well as overcommunicate. Finding the balance takes experience and sound judgement. Do not underestimate the task of communicating and the energy it takes to sustain effective communication of game's design during the lifetime of the project.

To help with this, lets discuss what kinds of communication are important in development.

HIGH-LEVEL VISION AND PILLARS

At the start of a project, the team needs to understand the vision of the game early and believe in its ability to become a successful commercial title. This process of selling the idea of the game, or the vision, is usually a public one done with the team as a whole and in front of key stakeholders. The designer's ability to articulate this vision is a key component of the team's confidence in the design.

This usually involves pitching or delivering the high-level concept or pillars of the game with supporting images and diagrams. The goal of this kind of communication is to give as much information about the game with as few words as possible. Rambling off into detailed explanations is to be avoided; focusing on single ideas that evoke a clear mental picture is preferable. Of course each studio has its own process for high-level pitching, but focusing on diagrams and images to communicate complex ideas is better than extensive text at this stage.

Find keywords that describe the vision as closely and concisely as possible, then use those terms consistently throughout the project material to tie it into earlier discussions and create a common language inside the team. These keywords must be reinforced and consistently defined to avoid confusing the team with terms that change meaning depending on who is speaking or get diluted over time. The design team is responsible for maintaining the message and its consistency, and if there is a change in definitions or vision, they should update these keywords and explain these changes.

Every studio has its own definition of what a game's "vision" should contain. The common factor is that it should be a concise explanation of the core components of the game expressed in a sentence or two. This is something that can be quickly transmitted to everyone in the team at any level, an "elevator pitch" if you will. This is more difficult than it sounds, because it needs to be impactful, convincing and use precise terms in as few words as possible.

The game pillars are usually three core gameplay components that underpin the project, but sometimes can include description of the player experience. The pillars can turn into production pillars as the project starts to solidify into preproduction. Game pillars are the main selling points of the idea around which production and design efforts are focused. So if there is some major technical innovation that will require considerable programmer effort, this should be one of the pillars. If there is a major narrative twist that has a serious impact on player impression and the art style, this should be one of the pillars. For example, if the player's point of view is unusual (they are a ghost, or animal, etc.), or they navigate by sound alone, or they play as a famous historical figure (gladiator, explorer, etc.).

The player "fantasy" is another way to define a pillar, what does the player do in the game, what is it that they become, why is that exciting and fun?

The pillars become reference points that anchor both task definitions and production estimations, in addition to being selling points and design references. Defining the pillars well serves the project in the long term and focuses development efforts on the priorities that make the game successful.

STAND-UPS

Scrum and agile methodologies are fond of the use of daily standing meetings where key people assigned to a project gather around their work area to discuss tasks, production issues or the daily workflow.

In theory, having everyone standing in a circle keeps everyone on topic and focuses the discussion in a minimum of time. Some teams like each person in the stand-up to describe their previous day's work and what they intend to accomplish today. This might not be useful to everyone in the meeting, especially if the group is large and you have other disciplines describing technical details that are not relevant to the others. It depends on the composition of the meeting and production needs, but the goal of the stand-up is for everyone to be able to learn something about the current set of tasks regardless of discipline.

Designer stand-up communication should be in the format of brief relevant information that updates the team on design decisions, results of iteration, the progress of current tasks and any

blockers or dependencies. Stand-ups should be as concise and directed as possible, the whole point of this format is to keep it short and relevant to everyone.

Design information should be limited to the progress of prototypes, current thinking within design and the results of iteration. Detailed design descriptions are to be avoided and clarifications should be taken offline in separate meetings if necessary.

Designers should also communicate any changes to features or updates to the documentation that would impact the current tasks. Do not assume that the team is keeping up with the current design documentation or that they are in the loop when major changes are announced. Overcommunication in this regard is beneficial.

MEETINGS

The dreaded meeting has become a much-maligned aspect of software development. It is true that badly structured and run meetings are productivity destroying and can become morale issues if such meetings are frequent and become a major tool for decision-making.

As a design leader, meetings are an important part of the process of communicating design, ironing out misunderstandings and deciding changes to the design. When properly used, meetings are the engine that drives smooth design development. The opposite is true when meetings are abused.

Here are some tips to make meetings a powerful tool for productivity:

1. **Have an agenda:** If you call a meeting, make sure you include a short, concise agenda that you will stick to. Sending the agenda ahead of time allows the people invited to the meeting to be properly prepared for it so they can bring the latest relevant information. Stick to the agenda and use it to keep the conversation focused on the discussion at hand. Do not be tempted to deviate unless it is important. Off-topic issues should be taken offline and discussed in separate conversations if necessary.

2. **Take notes:** A meeting is useless unless you record the conversation, the decisions made, action items and changes. Short notes that detail what was discussed, what the outcome of the discussion was and any further actions should be compiled at the end of each meeting, and sent out to the participants and any other stakeholders not present in the meeting. Without this process of record-keeping, the tendency is for people to forget what was discussed and decided, and the collective amnesia will result in more meetings about the very same issues over and over. It also ensures that decision-makers follow through and are accountable if there is ever confusion about why or when decisions were made.

3. **Invite the key stakeholders:** It is very tempting to invite as many people as possible to meetings in order to spread the information to as many team members as possible, but this practice inevitably prolongs the meeting or creates confusions when multiple voices want to be heard at the same gathering. Keep the list of invitees to those who really need to know the information discussed. Leads can pass on highlights of the discussion to their team. Senior managers can be invited if their decision is required, but otherwise can be kept in the loop with the notes. Inviting a representative from production to design meetings is also a good idea, since they can then react to decisions made after the meeting or interject if the discussion is outside of scope.

4. **Keep the duration of meetings under an hour:** From a psychologic standpoint, it is hard to discuss a topic productively for more than an hour. Beyond that time, the usefulness of a meeting starts to degrade exponentially. Think of 1 hour as your absolutely maximum limit, and if it needs to go beyond that, schedule another meeting later or set a new short time limit to quickly go over the remaining topics. If you are sticking to your agenda, this should help. If the meeting takes less time that you scheduled for, do not be

tempted to add more topics just to fill the time you booked. If you have covered all the agenda items in 5 minutes, end the meeting and get back to work. There is no obligation to keep a meeting going just because you scheduled more time than was needed to discuss the items.

EMAIL

A vital tool for transmitting design and keeping the team aware of game progress, emails from the design team should follow a standard format and have clear guidelines for content. Consider emails about game design to essentially be part of the design documentation. They should follow the content format that the rest of the design documentation uses.

When communicating news about design or new tasks, highlight in the email who is responsible for each item and which designer should be consulted for the different features. Most of the team will not necessarily know which designer handles which features, so ensuring they approach the right person when they need more detail really helps speed up their own internal process.

Emails should be flagged for importance and titles should be relevant to the content. Most people's inbox is flooded with emails so keeping your headlines concise and clear will make

sure that they reach the right people in time and any action items get attended to right away. As always, design must be clear and concise when communicating, even more so with emails as they are part of a vast stream of electronic communication that can become background noise during full development.

Things to avoid in emails: Do not enter back and forth discussions or debates in email. This tends to be counterproductive and leads to more confusion. Any complex discussion that requires explanation should be done face to face; a chain of emails will confuse the issue and possibly create even more misunderstanding. Designers must be careful how emails can be misinterpreted so use precise language and terms; reading the email to yourself from the receiver's perspective can help with wording and clarity. If your email gets a lengthy series of questions in response, avoid responding with another email if possible. A face-to-face conversation is better than back-and-forth correspondence, which tends to confuse, gets off the topic and delays in reaching a solution. It also can make a public spectacle of the conversation, which could lower the confidence of the team.

MESSAGE APPS

There are many different message apps for internal communication used in studios these days. While these have become essential tools for ensuring the transmission of information within the team, they need to be regulated and used wisely to avoid some of the productivity-destroying features of these tools. Design can get into a lot of trouble if messaging apps are not used properly, spreading confusion and causing potential wasted time clarifying misinterpretations caused by a badly worded message.

The key is to not design through messaging, this is a bad idea and will create a lot of misunderstandings. If you need to clarify or add missing detail to a design, do not use messaging apps to transmit this information, keep it in the design documentation or use email to update the team. First reason is you don't know who is actually reading or subscribed to a given thread. Second is that without context, your information may confuse or create more questions than it answers.

Furthermore, messaging apps are distracting, they are designed to catch the eye and generate traffic, much like social media. Constant prompts, pings and flashing messages can break your workflow if you allow the app to take over your desktop. A short browse through the settings will allow you to customize the notifications to maximize the value of the tool.

Pitfalls of messaging: Some people will be tempted to rely on messaging the design group rather than looking up answers in the design documentation. It is important to avoid supplanting or duplicating the documentation by providing off-the-cuff answers via messaging. There is a high likelihood that such quick replies will contradict the documentation or create confusion. As long as your documentation is up-to-date and current, you should always refer people to the right document rather than resort to the quick and easy fix of a message. Small questions that are more technical in nature are ok, but long questions should be answered fully by the design documents.

FACE TO FACE

You would think that something as simple and natural as a face-to-face conversation would need no explanation, but once again there are a few things to consider when you meet with a team mate to discuss design. First of all, it is always better to have at least three people in the room, to confirm that the topics discussed were all understood. Second, do not design on the fly in such conversations, always try to document your design, publish it and then discuss what you wrote. Even if it ends up getting changed, it is better to document your intention rather than throw ideas out for people to interpret any way they want. If you want to discuss alternatives, make sure that the person you are speaking with understands that it is up for discussion. If you do not make it clear, they may go back to their team or group and repeat what you said as if it's final design.

Because you cannot be present in every design conversation, always make sure that what you tell people is accurate, official and part of the design consensus. If not, they will transmit incorrect information that will spread through the team, and you will have to clean up the mess if it does not match the final design.

A good habit to make sure this does not happen is to write a short email to the person you just spoke to with a quick recap of what was discussed. It also allows others to be in the loop and sanity check the information.

COMMUNICATION INTEGRITY

Earning the respect of the team as a designer requires professional discipline and integrity. Designers enjoy a degree of freedom that other disciplines don't, and the team may grow to reset your freedom if they feel it is misused. By "freedom", I mean: designers can choose features, their job is more creative and expressive of their inner preferences, and they can set their own deadlines and outcomes in many ways. This freedom comes at a price of course; designers must be correct about their hunches and responsible for results that do not meet gameplay expectations. It is a good practice to earn that freedom by being more disciplined with your time and hold yourself to a higher professional standard in your day-to-day interactions. This will pay off when the results of your work come in and it gets judged by the entire team. If you have been professionally sloppy, casual about how you communicate or disorganized in your work, the final results of your designs will be judged in that light. When the team has to solve problems or push features that are not fully mature, their lack of confidence will affect their effort and the results.

Be respectful of your colleagues in all your communications, resist the urge to complain or gossip about other team members even if they are difficult or unprofessional. If you engage in this kind of negativity, you will gain a reputation as a complainer and nobody wants to be around one. Be constructive in bringing up issues and raise them with the individual in question upfront.

If you can't do that, solve the problem yourself or move on. If you allow issues that you can't change to continue, they occupy your mindshare and take up your emotional energy which will eventually affect your work, lower your energy levels and create a vibe around you that people will want to avoid. Designers must be optimistic and positive, after all you are selling a dream and should act accordingly.

Own your mistakes, admit your failures and move on. It is generally a good practice and will lead to your professional growth and it will greatly improve the team's respect. Acting as if you are infallible or afraid to admit your errors will colour people's perception of your maturity and ego. Designers already are considered somewhat childlike because their work is so much linked to imagination and child's play; do not reinforce this perception by being professionally immature.

Give credit where it is due, do not claim authorship for every bright idea or success, let others shine and give them the accolades that make them feel good about contributing to design and making features. There will be plenty of credit to spread around if you finish the game and it launches successfully. Do not claim credit; allow others to assign it to you based on your good work and talent.

Pick your design battles carefully. Do not be tempted to fight every time you can't have what you want in design. Resisting changes to your work could be a sign of being precious, you must allow others to infuse your work with their ideas and respond to their feedback. But do not mistake this with being completely open to every change that is suggested. If you bend to every suggestion, you can't build anything coherent or with a strong identity. You must fight for your design but fight the important battles, not every battle. By fighting I mean use logical arguments and back it up with proof provided by prototyping and testing.

Other things to consider: Think before you speak (and email). Emails can be easily misconstrued, so choose your wording carefully and re-read it from the recipient's perspective. The tone of your communication will have a big impact on how well your ideas will be received. Be consistent with your language and your terms. Be available to answer questions and clarify, be passionate but objective, admit it if you don't understand your goals or the constraints.

COMMUNICATING WITH THE OTHER DISCIPLINES

Game development is a juggling act, design is never fully in control of all the variables of a project and the other disciplines suffer from their own set of unknowns. Having a sense of what the other disciplines must deal with gives you a better understanding of how your design may be affected and how to adapt.

Communicating with Production Teams

Production has a general idea of a schedule and a budget at the beginning of a project, but this often changes based on market innovations and the needs of the company. New information about the progress of key features, staffing issues, publisher expectations, studio management expectations, results of testing,

etc., can lead to changes and new features. In other words, producers deal with all these variables and incorporate them into a constantly revised production plan.

As a designer, your features will have to navigate these changes and you must adapt to new production conditions constantly. Adapting without upsetting the delicate balance of your feature-set, in whatever state it may be in, is a difficult skill to master. One of the ways you can make this easier is to keep production in the loop about features and design goals. Invite them to design discussions on major feature decisions, ask for their input on how to adapt design to the schedule, keep them looped into emails and major decisions about design. When production is informed about the state of design, they can take that into their production discussions with management. They can advocate for your features before a final decision is made and speak to the value of some of the completed work.

Some possible publisher scenarios you might have to deal with: budget change, schedule change, feature priority change, increase content, decrease content, add a platform, change engine and pivot to a new genre. These changes are generally communicated via production, which will have already presented or negotiated the impact of these changes. Sometimes design is asked to provide more information before making such decisions, but not always. Either way, when these kinds of changes are made, production will ask for an assessment of the design changes required to adapt the game. This does not always mean cutting features, it could simply mean how much change to the design is required to absorb the new schedule.

You may have been given approval to build a major complex feature that will take a long time to prove out, and then be asked to keep the feature but adapt it to a much smaller period of development. Best way to deal with this is to have a B version of the feature already in mind when you design it. Designing a feature with a B version allows you to retain consistency with your other features, without requiring a major rework or rebalance.

It is an inevitable part of creative partnerships that creative leads have differences over priorities or vision. Production can be the arbiter that keeps the balance of power without itself becoming a creative arbiter. Production should remain neutral in these discussions and maintain the focus and priorities of each team. They should be able to communicate sensitive feedback from different members of the team while keeping a healthy relationship within the team.

Producers should know the difference between healthy, constructive discussions and unproductive arguments. I have seen inexperienced producers interfering in perfectly normal design discussions that they felt were unproductive. This is a grave sin, producers are not there to judge the merits of design discussions, that is for the leads to determine. Producers are there to judge whether work is moving forward and whether important decisions are being made and what actions need to be taken.

Communicating with Art Teams

At the start of a project, there is usually a period of exploration where the art teams look for the right visual style for environments, characters and user interface (UI). Animation budgets and modelling requirements are being estimated based on the design pillars and vision, but these are rough drafts and prone to change quite a lot.

Design is heavily invested in these discussions because the art group's decisions will put some important constraints on what you can do in the game. The art leads will be exploring various ideas initially that will gradually evolve into a unified art direction. It is important that design does not try to lead this discussion or push for a certain direction unless you are expected to be part of that discussion. Art teams need the freedom to explore before any major budget or schedule constraints are imposed, joining that discussion rather than leading it gives them the attitude they need to do their best thinking. This is a critical discussion because once a visual direction and style is chosen, it is hard to reverse beyond a certain point in development. It will also have repercussions on design that are hard to predict at the early stages of a project.

The team itself will often debate which direction they prefer, generating a lot of potentially different options to choose from. Only when these discussions have happened can the art departments begin to give accurate estimates on the production implications of the different choices. As a designer, you need to understand the art direction options and what it means for your features.

Art direction is usually a big deal to publishers and studio management who sometimes express an opinion on what they don't think fits the project. This can sometimes come down to avoiding a visual style that may be too similar to another game. Trying to stand out in an increasingly crowded market is becoming more difficult with each year; finding a unique visual style is one good way to gain attention in a market that is flooded with some very distinct looking titles. As hardware improvements increase the visual fidelity of games, art directors are under added pressure to find new styles. If you present design as an ally in this quest, rather than just another set of constraints they have to deal with, you can find a compromise between your needs and the demands of art.

Communicating with Tech Teams

The technology aspect of game development can be a very tricky dragon to tame for a game designer. Depending on many factors, a game project could have a well-known and well-supported engine to work with or there may be the requirement to build something from scratch based on brand new tech. There are advantages/disadvantages to both of these situations from a design perspective.

A well-worn engine with a programming team that understands it will be able to quickly produce a stable set of features. However, such technology may have legacy limitations that

impose certain restrictions on your design. Engines can be good at performing some processes and not so great at others. You may only find out later in development about these limitations, potentially killing a major feature of your design. It is hard to predict how well the engine will handle all the features together once they are built; there may be a persistent issue that causes instability due to incompatibility between a key feature and the way the engine works. Trying to modify an engine to make it backwards compatible with such a feature is a risky option most of the time.

Few teams these days have the mandate to build an engine along with a game, most of the time it is a case of taking an existing engine and investing heavily in tools to develop a specific type of game. This requires the game design to be fairly advanced in order to be able to create specs for tool teams. These situations can be uncharted waters with many pitfalls. Providing you can convince programming to support the vision, the advantage is that you get to build the tools and features you want, to your specifications, giving your initial design direction more flexibility and perhaps allowing you to do something really unique and fresh.

Communicating the design intentions and negotiating the tech requirements require you to be open to being educated on the technical feasibility of your features. It is unwise to not compromise on certain technical limitations, especially if they are going to become a major risk in proving the core gameplay. Build the game in collaboration with the tech team and you are far less likely to run into major technical roadblocks.

One of the biggest mistakes an inexperienced team makes is in believing that its tech planning is accurate. Unless there are some solid veteran tech leads who have planned on the same technology before, it is highly likely that any early planning is quite subjective. Unless the team is honest about what they do not know and what they are simply guessing at, the plan is only going to get you in trouble. Technology bets are always the biggest wild card, and this is where experienced technical leads are vital. If your team is not familiar with the technology or generally inexperienced, the production plan should take into account the possibility of a wide margin of error on time estimates and your design should include alternative plans in the event some features prove not to be technically feasible after prototyping. In an ideal situation, you have expert tech leads on your project but in reality, this type of experience is rare and in high demand, so expect to be surprised and prepare to adapt.

COMMUNICATING DESIGN TASKS

Most projects use some sort of tracking tool such as Jira. Regardless of the tool your studio uses, it's only as accurate and useful as the users make it. Most projects seldom use their tracking tools to their full potential for various reasons, chief among them, human nature and the different needs of each department. In theory, tracking tools should give you a full picture on the rate of progress and productivity in the team, but in practice the data each team provides to the tracking tool is usually of varying degrees of quality and accuracy. In addition, every studio enforces tracking tool use to varying degrees of diligence. In my experience, as the data becomes less accurate, teams tend to start ignoring the tracking tool and in some of the worst cases, even abandon it as it becomes too large a task to clean up all the information and overhaul the tracking data. I have heard of production teams going to each person's desk one by one in the morning to update each of their Jira tasks properly in order to prevent this. It may sound too time-consuming to enforce this kind of bookkeeping, but the alternative is much worse.

Production teams can get a lot of out-tracking tools if they enforce a standard by which they are used and push the team to maintain that standard throughout the project. Enforcement means updating individual tasks regularly, using the right categories and naming conventions, setting a clear standard of what the priority scale is and assignment rules. They don't let tasks or bugs get hoarded by one lead, they make sure old tasks are properly estimated and closed; they set strict criteria for reporting and information requirements for bugs.

One of the challenges for a production team is that each discipline uses the tool differently according to the nature of their work. Artists use different conventions than programmers, tasks are estimated differently and the steps to complete a task may involve more dependencies or more than one person. Assuming each team has its own producer, these different usages can be standardized into a single common format that takes into account each team's needs for the tool while translating accurately into a common schedule relevant data language.

This can be less of an issue with smaller projects and teams; however, losing the ability to accurately plan for long term opens a Pandora's box of project problems, the worst of which is entering a twilight zone of rolling deadlines that do not seem to visibly progress the project in a specific direction. You don't want to be designing under those conditions, trust me, whatever "freedom" you may think this may give you as a designer is greatly offset by the chaos it brings. Design without firm deadlines and constraints is rarely successful, and the game industry is littered with examples of projects where design was allowed to float in a nebulous sea of missed deadlines that never shipped, or if they did, it was under years of tortuous conditions that saw a lot of churn, months of crunch and a failed product at the end.

Accurately assessing design tasks is difficult. Production may require detail that is difficult to provide accurately, but you should try to give good estimates whenever possible. Experience brings a lot of clarity in this area, but one way to tackle the complex job of estimating design tasks is by simply breaking down each design job into its component parts.

Types of Design Tasks

- **Concept research:** In preproduction, or even before any budget or schedule exists, designers sometimes have the luxury of time to explore high-level design ideas for their next future project. Depending on the studio, this process is labelled differently, but my preferred term is "research" because I feel this best describes the kind of work involved. Concept research involves a lot of discussions, a lot of reading, watching videos and movies and much pondering. This is difficult to schedule for, or even track. The results are onerous to evaluate from a production standpoint, when is this task considered complete for example? What is considered a finished concept? Instead of trying to answer these questions, the best approach is to give concept research a firm deadline, and let the designers do what they can within that time frame. This could be from a week to a few months, depending on the scope of the project. This allows the designers the freedom to just go through their own process to find the idea and articulate it, with the understanding of when speculation and exploration must end and whatever concept has been arrived should be translated into a polished presentation that can be reviewed by the powers that be. It is not very useful to track this process beyond a deadline, unless your design team is inexperienced and needs the occasional check-in to ensure that the process is moving forward.

The concept document may be accompanied by early prototypes, art concepts, in some studios some early gameplay may be required, but that depends entirely on the technology, the studio and the time available. At the minimum though, the concept research phase should produce a vision document. A description of the suggested contents of a vision document is described in this chapter.

- **Design documentation:** This task can persist from preproduction through to alpha stages. Each feature of the game needs to be designed and described in terms of intentions, mechanics and system descriptions. The level of detail for these documents should limit itself at just describing the overall intention and main features of the game.

  All design documents coming from a design team should follow the same formatting, style and layout system. Having a standard format helps the team navigate the documentation and keeps the quality high. Enforcing a standard makes it more likely that the rest of the team will read the design documents, a process that is already difficult (it may surprise the reader that development teams do not like reading design documents or rarely read them completely!). Anything you can do to improve the readability, clarity and interest of the documentation (a few memes here and there never hurt) will increase the likelihood that your fellow developers will read your documents!

Design documentation is hard to estimate, since the process of creativity is hard to predict, and the design is usually informed through discoveries in prototyping and iteration. The recommended approach with design documentation is to assume there will be a three step process: draft, first pass and final approved version.

Draft Design Document

Draft versions are quick designs that describe the main intention of the feature and its most significant components from a production point of view. Each design document should have the following content:

- **Intention:** It is the main purpose of the feature from the point of view of the player. What is the fun of this feature, how is the player supposed to react to this gameplay and how does this add to the overall game experience. This section is short and to the point. It is basically a justification for why the feature should be made.

- **Design description:** The main body of the document should go through the description of the feature step by step. Include pictures, diagrams and charts as necessary to visually pepper the document with visual reference points, and to enhance the description with visuals that will explain better than text alone. I recommend adding one picture per page (does not have to be large or detailed) to give the reader a reference point as to where they are in the document, and to illustrate the topic described. For example, if a page is describing melee combat, a picture of two characters wrestling might be a good choice. The design description should be easy to read, organized and with numerical reference points. For example:

Melee combat design:

1. Hand-to-hand combat

2. Sword combat

3. Push and kick attacks

The use of this type of layout makes it easier to reference which part of the document you are in when reviewing it with the team, especially when you are not all in the same room.

The design description can't cover every aspect of a feature, so don't try to make an exhaustive list in this type of documentation. It will make these documents too cumbersome and dense to adequately obtain the necessary information. For design details, there is another type of documentation I call "feature descriptions", which is explained further in this chapter.

- **Designer's notes:** The last part of the document should describe the philosophy of the feature and any potential alternative versions, such as a less complex B version. It can include thoughts and ideas for future exploration, the rationale the designer used or anything else that might illustrate better the idea behind the design and the different choices made. Sometimes, it is good for the team to see the rationale of the design and understand why certain choices were made. It can answer a lot of questions that will otherwise crop up in meetings down the line, and give the team confidence in the designer's thought process and decisions.

  The draft version of the design is for internal review within the design team. It is ok to show a draft design to the rest of the team with the clear understanding that it's a draft and subject to lots of changes, therefore not yet something to work off. Making drafts public can help build consensus and give the team discussion topics of their own so they can prepare questions and answers when the document is ready for review.

Draft designs are discussed within the creative leadership of the team and then go through a formal approval process to become a first pass version.

First Pass

This version of the design document includes all the feedback and changes produced from the review of the draft. The purpose is to create a document that is ready for public consumption. The team can read it knowing that most of its contents are going to make it into the game. Its contents are still theoretical, the design document is not the source for people to go to in order to get their tasks, but it gives the teams working on gameplay features a clear idea of the intention of these features, their main components and their implications on production.

The first pass is reviewed with the senior leads in the team, who often have their own feedback, changes or other comments that must be resolved by the design team before the design can be considered final.

Final Approved Version

These are designs that have been reviewed, changed, updated and approved by the senior leadership of the team. This means that all the leads have had a chance to review them and give their own input from the perspective of their discipline. This can happen either through a meeting to discuss the design with all major stakeholders in the room, or it can be an ongoing discussion managed by producers who get sign off from each department on their own time.

Once a design document is approved and final, it goes into the repository of design where anyone on the team can access it knowing that it has been discussed, debated, reviewed and approved as official and final. The design team is responsible for maintaining these to varying degrees from then on. Design documents are useful up to a point in production. Beyond alpha, they become more obsolete, as cuts start to have impact and major features are reworked. In an ideal world, design has the time to update each approved design document with any changes to these features but in reality, it would take too much time for a design team to maintain and carry out their other development duties. As the game enters beta stage, most design teams are overwhelmed with much more important tasks than documentation.

This is one of the reasons why teams should rely on a third layer of design documents, the feature description (FD).

Feature Descriptions

These types of documents go into a level of detail that is useful for all disciplines, in a format that is simple, easy to review and with exact information with minimum language. The best way to describe these documents is design pseudo code.

Pioneered at Ubisoft, this type of documentation came out of the need to communicate precise feature information to very large teams with varying degrees of English language comprehension. The idea was to cut back on the prose of design documents and distil them into their most basic components so that each discipline can extract the exact tasks each of them needs to work on to complete the feature.

But the magic does not stop there, the FD format is also a functional production list and a regression list for quality assurance (QA).

The FD format uses a spreadsheet, such as the Excel file format. The typical FD will have the following sections:

- **Title:** Feature Name

- **Project:** Which game project does this feature belong to.

- **Designer:** The name of the designer who owns this feature that everyone can contact for questions, details or changes to this document. This designer is responsible for updating this document throughout the project.

- **Intention:** This paragraph repeats the main intention of the feature from a player's perspective. This can use a section from the design documentation or can be a more condensed summary of what the feature does and how it fits into the overall game. This places the information in the document in the proper context.

- **Description:** This is the main body of the document and should consist of line-by-line detail of exactly how the feature functions, from a mechanical point of view.

Each line describes a single function of the feature. Following are few examples:

- How to activate the feature (button press, interaction, etc.)?

- How long do any gameplay effects last (duration)?

- How much area of the environment does the feature affect?

- Any AI behaviour associated with the feature.

- Any changes to AI behaviour based on player use of the feature.

- Any changes to inventory contents or active items.

- The UI elements for this feature.

- Menu items.

- Changes to progression.

- Combat effects, buffs, debuffs, cooldowns and interrupts.

- Any animation associated with the feature.

- Any 3D assets associated with the feature.

- Any particle effects or visual feedback.

- Any audio effects or audio feedback.

Feature Description (example)

		Design notes	Production notes	Status	QA
Title	Gameplay Feature Description Document				
Project	Your game				
Designer	Your name				
Feature Summary	This document is a method of managing design feature documentation in a way that is both easy to maintain and easy to understand by all disciplines. It also functions as a production tracking tool and a regression test plan. In this section the designer describes in one or two paragraphs the design intention of the feature, to give context.	This column is reserved for any designer notes regarding intentions, references, vision or progress of iteration. The purpose is to clarify for the other disciplines and give some visibility into the design decision process.	Each task is linked in this column for reference	This column shows progress of the feature with a colour code system shown below	QA can confirm the testing of each finished feature in this column and link tickets.
Functionality	This section is a line by line description of how the feature functions			Not Started = RED	
	It is written in the format of pseudocode			In Progress = Yellow	
	Each line is a description of one single step in the function of the feature			Complete = Green	
	The text is meant to be as concise and simple as possible				
	The language used avoids imprecise terms such as "should", "possible", "sorta" etc..				
	First part should describe controls or activation mechanics of the feature				
	When necessary controler button or keymapping is included for each platform				
	Any UI feedback mechanics associated with the feature are detailed				
	Any other feedback (VFX or SFX) are described				
	Any inventory management or menu interactions are described				
	Functionality for gameplay developers is described in detail with logic flow				
	The designer goes through the mechanics of the feature and works out implementation details line by line				
	In a step by step format the designer describes how the entire feature functions with edge cases and exceptions				
	If a specific part of the feature is yet to be determined (TBD) is used until the information is updated				
	If time values are mentioned the are written as (X)s for seconds				
	If other numerical values are detailed the are placed in (#)				
	If a numerical value can change based on iteration it is written in RED so that the value is accessible to design				
	If a new line is added to the document it is highlighted in yellow				
	Any parts of the feature that are cut are highlighted in red rather than deleted for continuity and tracking				
3D	Each model needed to support this feature is described in simple language				
	If available references are attached in the design notes				
	This is not an art guide, just a requirement list				
Animation	Any animations needed to support the feature are described one by one				
	Walking, climbing and similar simple descriptions are sufficient				
UI	Any UI or screen effects are detailed here if relevant				
Audio	Any sound FX or speech recordings are described				
Menu	Described any menu buttons or pages needed for the feature				
Network	Any multiplayer or network support for the feature is described here such as ranked stats, etc...				
Store	Any storefront support is detailed here				
Achievements	Any achievements are listed here for each supported platform				

DESIGN COMMUNICATION THROUGH EACH STAGE OF DEVELOPMENT

Preproduction

The designer has different jobs for each stage of a development project. Preproduction is usually the start of development with a small core team of key leads and designers who are assembled to start defining the early stages of a project that has been given the green light by upper management. Sometimes, however, there is a bit of give and take required before official green light is given, and the results of preproduction work leads to a yes or no from either publishers or studio management or both.

Design work in this stage of development as mentioned before is not to detail systems or clearly define all gameplay. It is closer to research that should lead to answering the following questions:

Core Experience

What is the core game experience? What genre(s) is it closest to and what are the core pillars of gameplay? Refer to the more detailed explanation earlier in this chapter.

A key question that this should answer is what is the innovation of this game? How does the design improve upon previous similar titles or what new unique feature are you creating?

There are several ways to innovate:

1. **New game technology:** There are many famous examples of games that were the first to bring a new technology to the market. Some examples of tech innovations could be a uniquely detailed environment destruction system, the ability to support more active AI than previous games or massive detailed environments. There are many possibilities since games keep pushing the boundaries of what is feasible. If you are planning on innovating on a game technology, you should demonstrate in the pitch how this

technology would work, how it improves the game land-scape and who in the team will have the skills to create this tech.

2. **New gameplay:** Are you bringing a unique combination of features or a brand new feature to the market? Are you aiming for an extra hardcore or super casual experience? The pitch should explain the appeal of these features and explain generally how they would work.

3. **New visuals:** Does your game has unique art direction or character design? Who will be delivering this artistic vision and what do early concepts of these visuals look like? How does this art direction sell the game concept or the setting?

Project Scope

What is the scope and budget? How much money, time and peo-ple will be allocated to development? This is almost entirely out of design's hands, but each factor has to be reflected in the design of the core game experience and platform strategy (see below).

This simply means you must design within budget, with the human resources available in the time given. Think of each of these three factors as content modulators. The more of each that you have, the more content "volume" you have to work with.

You can visualize this in the graph below. X is your staffing plan, Y is your budget and Z is time.

Each factor is somewhat interrelated, if you have more money you can hire more staff or hire more experienced staff or spend longer on development. Overall budget is the defining factor of what level of publishing you are aiming the game for: Indie, early access, crowdfunded, AA, AA+ or AAA.

Needless to say, the more of everything you have, the more con-tent you can create, defined by the triangular volume S, for Scope.

Designing within the scope of the project is the main job of preproduction and it takes experience to understand what is

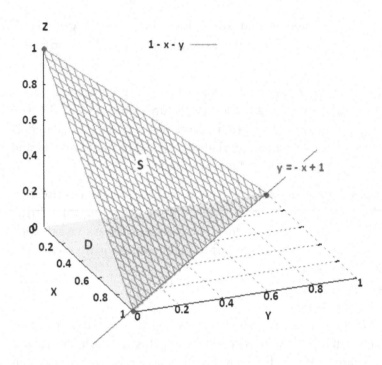

within and outside of the scope of your project. It really helps when all of the disciplines are involved in the conversation with management and publishing.

As the designer, your main goal during this phase is to gain consensus between all of the stakeholders through a series of back and forth conversations where you act as the intermediary, gathering the facts from each group and integrating them into the design plan. The accuracy of your design plan will depend on how well you communicate the scope to each group and refine it during preproduction.

Audience

What is the gamer demographic you are aiming this experience at? Is it a hardcore or casual audience, is it aimed at younger or older gamers? How is this reflected in the game design and content?

Technology

Which game engine will be used? What are the choices, if any? Will the technology support the type of features you want to create? How well developed are the tools for content creation?

Technology is a huge factor in design, it may limit certain types of gameplay or make developing them very time consuming. This should be accounted for in the design.

Market Landscape

What is the competitive landscape for this audience and genre? Who are the key players and the top titles that your game will be compared to? What are the minimum core features these market leaders have and how do your features compare against them? How much are you meeting market expectations on content and how are you innovating? Another way to answer this is to ask yourself, why would I play this game if I have already played the leading competitors title?

Publishing Strategy

What is the platform/publishing strategy? Which consoles, if any, will you develop the game on. Each platform requires its own specialized control set, art optimization, code optimization, design balancing, technical requirements checklist (TRC) compliance and storefront integration. How does your game leverage the potential of each platform chosen?

If releasing on PC, which storefronts? As competition becomes more fierce on PC, this decision could lock you into a specific ecosystem as some storefronts seek out exclusive releases. Fortunately, these complex decisions are not usually left to the design team, but designers will be asked to inform this decision with their own estimation of which platform(s) are the most suitable for the type of game being made?

Monetization

Part of the publishing strategy is monetization: free to play (F2P), in-game purchases or traditional pricing model. This decision impacts the design to a major degree, features designed for F2P are often not palatable to audiences of traditional commercial release and vice versa. In-game purchases are ok in the context of F2P games, but not so well received in full-priced titles. Subscription games require a minimum content bar on release that must be updated regularly with new downloadable content. This decision impacts not just how you will make the game profitable, but how much content needs to be built for the initial release and post release. A game that is designed to make all of its revenue on a single release is organized differently than a game that will earn its revenue over time, based on capturing a strong initial audience then selling more content over an extended period.

Preproduction usually ends when the major stakeholders are satisfied with the core design, and all of the key questions listed above are answered. This could take anywhere from a month to half a year, depending on the project scope.

At the end of preproduction, there is usually a vision document, a pitch document and the initial core game design documents complete with concept art, sometimes a show reel, prototype assets or, in some cases, a working prototype with some key early game mechanics. It really depends on the comfort level of the senior management team; the more risk averse it is, the longer the preproduction period.

Prototyping

Depending on the studio and the track record of the team, some management will require a working prototype to test the team's ability to deliver on the initial core game. A more experienced team with a good track record may be asked to go straight into production; new teams working with new technology will probably produce an initial prototype with low-quality assets to test the concept and the team's ability to deliver it.

Your job during prototyping is to inform the team of the priority assets that you will need to create a working prototype within the given timeline. This is a negotiation process, but it should be based on selecting the most representative elements of gameplay that can be quickly built and tested for iteration.

Iteration is a process of trying something, evaluating it as a team, critiquing the results, refining and then trying it again. Your job as a designer here is to provide information to the team so they can build and test things quickly. You are setting priorities for what needs to be built and designing the gameplay data that will give the most accurate representation of the gameplay experience you are looking for.

The second part of iteration is getting good feedback. You must take the latest version of the prototype to the key stakeholders and ask for their testing feedback. You then prioritize which issues will be addressed in the next version of the prototype. Your main job is to keep that cycle going, with the assistance of production that will help you drive it and provide the resources.

Once the prototype is judged to be a good representation of the core concept and everyone is confident in the team's ability to deliver the rest of it, the game goes into production. Each studio has its own criteria for evaluating this stage, and some studios will cancel a project if the prototype is not satisfactory. If you are on such a project, there are some valuable lessons to be learned from this kind of situation. Focus on trying to figure those lessons out and try to grow as a designer. Every failure is a valuable learning opportunity.

Production

- **First playable/vertical slice:** Once a prototype has been approved to go into production, the first milestone for the team is to reach a first playable version of the game. This is sometimes called a "vertical slice" or some teams consider them different stages. First playable is usually only focused on core gameplay rather than content, so the core gameplay is demonstrated at a higher degree of polish and with a sample art pass. Vertical slice will add an hour or more of playable content, with sample environments, a few representative AI examples, some progression and examples of the game economy loop, if any.

Each of these milestones will refine the game concept, change some of the design and realign the project towards new goals based on lessons learned. As a designer your job is to be flexible and respond to feedback during the milestones. Adapt the design and keep the process of refining the game as you did in the prototyping phase. Stay open to feedback and be willing to quickly drop features or mechanics that do not work well enough or that take too much production resources to polish.

Alpha

The definition of alpha varies from studio to studio, but generally this is where most of development is focused. All core systems and gameplay are built during alpha, including all environments. Art assets are prepared but not fully integrated until the end, along with story/narrative/cut scenes.

Your job during alpha is to continue refining the gameplay that was demonstrated in the vertical slice, and adding new systems and content in such a way to keep that experience consistently good. Keeping the game on track when new systems are being added is a difficult balancing act and it will be important to manage your time well enough so that you can be available to provide direction to all teams working on your features. This can be the most intensive stage of a project, where a lot of things can become confusing and the direction of the game can change based on some unforeseen obstacles.

The key concept here for the designer is consistency. Whereas in prototyping flexibility was important, in alpha you must maintain a consistent picture of the final game as it is being put together by the entire team. You have to understand what everyone is building and when you need to fix, cut and add. Responding to feedback as always is important, but keeping a consistent vision for the progress of gameplay is particularly important at this stage as it will be easy to get off-track or for competing visions to creep in. While everyone will be very busy building stuff, you as the designer will have a heads-up perspective enabling you to keep an eye on the final results of all this work. It is important to communicate when things are not on track and indicate how to get them back on.

Staying on track during alpha requires effort, but it will greatly assist you to have good time management, discipline in your work and some of the communication techniques described in this chapter. Remember that production is here to help; they are a resource for you when things are getting overwhelming or communication quality starts to become difficult to maintain. Do not suffer in silence, it is your job to raise red flags and ask for help when necessary.

Keeping up with documentation in alpha may seem time-consuming, especially if features change rapidly, but if you are maintaining the minimalist feature descriptions in spreadsheet format, this will greatly assist you in bookkeeping. It is especially important to update these design documents in large teams because it is the only way you can guarantee that all the correct information is available to whomever may be working on your features. There will be usually several people working on one feature and they may change depending on production needs. One programmer may be working on a system for a month, and then is replaced by another. A good way to maintain continuity between their work is to keep your feature descriptions up-to-date.

Beta

All gameplay systems are in the build and most of the art assets are fully integrated. The game is supposed to be feature complete at this stage; any gameplay systems that are not fully integrated are usually cut at this point. The focus is on closing development, rather than building content. There is still much work before release and design will be busy with polish and balancing. QA is verifying everything is functional and asset complete while building a bug list that everyone will be working off of for the next milestones.

Ideally, the programming team is just focused on bug fixing during this stage. They will need a list of priority fixes from design to start on, which you must update as frequently as possible. Bugs that prevent you from playing the game will get first attention, such as crashes and game locks. Major game systems that are not functioning properly should be next on the list. This includes visual or feedback bugs that prevent the feature from being understood or undermine the experience. Sometimes, a very small bug can make a feature seem completely broken, like a sound effect not playing. Don't underestimate how these seemingly minor bugs can undermine the overall experience, so put them high on the priority list. Easy fixes should not be left until the end if they are preventing the gameplay from reaching full potential. These bugs are sometimes called "production value" or polish bugs.

Balancing and tweaking is the other major job of design during this stage, and it is a vital final stage of designing the game. For system designers, the gameplay data that controls the gameplay experience is your responsibility in order to create the most polished gaming experience. Some development studios take this facet of design for granted, the data has been often in place for a long time and not all of it has come from the design team. In some cases when a system is built, gameplay programmers will include some placeholder data just to make sure it is functioning. Animators may set the timings for various animation sequences to values that are arbitrary, just to make the animation look ok. They are not operating under any set of guidelines because design often is busy with many tasks during alpha or is even unaware of the asset in question. Oftentimes, this data remains in place for many milestones and it becomes "official", and nobody bothers to change it or look at it again. The team gets so used to this data that they start to believe that this is the intended design, and sometimes changing it will raise alarm. In order for you to fully polish the final experience, you must rein in all of this data; both your own and any placeholder values from other sources and do a final balancing and tweak pass to refine the experience.

The ideal way to do this effectively is outside of the editor, you should have a copy of all the major gameplay data in a spreadsheet or similar format that permits you to look at the whole balance picture in a comparative way that allows for quick analysis. Trying to iterate in the editor is time-consuming and does not give you a proper sense of the big picture, especially overall balancing. When you have obtained the key values from the editor and set up a proper big picture view of this data, you may start to see anomalies or imbalances quickly. Some values will be inconsistent with others, there will be corrupt data (really strange numbers with lots of decimal places that actually serve no purpose) and junk data (values that do not work or do anything, yet they have to be set at this value in order for the system to work, don't ask.).

This data pass is crucial for balancing combat, economies, loot items and progression. There is a lot of information and balancing is a delicate process; it is easy to change one set of values and find out later that it throws something else out of balance. One way to avoid this is to take an incremental approach and change one value at a time before setting the final value. For example, if testing determines that a specific weapon is too powerful you may be tempted to go into the weapon values and change a few of them at the same time (nerfing). Avoid doing this because it makes it harder to determine the real cause of the imbalance. Try tweaking one value at a time, review the result, and then change another if necessary. So for example, instead of lowering damage, speed and raising the cost of the weapon, try just doing one of those things first and see if that fixes the imbalance.

Balancing level environments is another important task in beta, and there are many good sources of information and advice on this vast topic that I will not try to reproduce here. I will mention though that if you are changing gameplay, it is a good idea to inform level designers who are going to need to understand those changes to adapt their own balance in their levels. If a type of AI is now much tougher because of a balancing pass you made, level design will need to adjust the population of these AI to reflect their new difficulty level. As always, communicating what you are doing that may have repercussions on other people's work is simply good work etiquette, and balance changes in beta can be quite unwelcome surprises requiring a lot of rework if not notified in time.

Design documentation should be maintained to help QA keep their regression test plans accurate, once again I refer you to the FD documentation. In beta, there tend to be many cuts to the game, both large and small. Keeping a history of the cuts helps QA keep its test plans accurate and prevents false bugs from clogging the backlog.

CONCLUSION

Every discipline in game development uses a tool in the process of building their own contribution to a game development project. Producers use scheduling tools and charts, programmers work with engines, artists use drawing software, etc. Designers use language, communication is the principle tool through which you work with the other teams. You need to be just as precise with this tool as the other disciplines are with their own.

A good analogy for creating video games is the music industry. When a band of musicians get together, they each play different instruments but the result is a harmonious song. If we were to stretch this analogy further you could say that, for example, producers are the band managers who book the shows and make sure the band starts on time, gets paid, etc. Similarly, programmers are the drummers, laying the foundation for the song and keeping everyone else on the beat. Artists could be the guitar players. (Of course this is a simple analogy, so please don't try to draw any direct inference between the choice of instrument and the actual developer discipline!) In this example, designers are the singers. And no, not because they are the stars or the most flamboyant performers, there is no implication of them being "front men" or any such prestige. This is because like a singer, they use their voice; there is no intermediary between the singer and the audience. Your voice is all you, there is no instrument coming between you and the audience who can hear every nuance and note of sincerity and clarity.

So, communicate as if you were singing in front of an audience that can hear every note coming from your soul.

Index

Printed in the United States
by Baker & Taylor Publisher Services

Printed in the United States
by Baker & Taylor Publisher Services